THOUGHT
CHOICE
ACTION

DECISION-MAKING THAT RELEASES
THE HOLY SPIRIT'S POWER

Ron Sandison

ELECTIO PUBLISHING
first century principles.
a twenty-first century approach.

Thought, Choice, Action
By Ron Sandison

Copyright 2018 by Ron Sandison. All rights reserved.
Cover Design by eLectio Publishing

ISBN-13: 978-1-63213-524-7

Published by eLectio Publishing, LLC

Little Elm, Texas

http://www.eLectioPublishing.com

5 4 3 2 1 eLP 22 21 20 19 18

Printed in the United States of America.

The eLectio Publishing creative team is comprised of: Kaitlyn Campbell, Emily Certain, Lori Draft, Jim Eccles, Sheldon James, and Christine LePorte.

Publisher's Note

The publisher does not have any control over and does not assume any responsibility for author or third-party websites or their content.

Endorsements for
Thought, Choice, Action

Thought, Choice, Action is filled with good theology and good sense. Ron's personal testimony is worth the value of the book.

~ Dr. Walter C. Kaiser Jr., the Colman M. Mockler distinguished Professor Emeritus of Old Testament and former President of Gordon-Conwell Theological Seminary 1997-2006

Ron Sandison has masterfully blended history, Scripture and contemporary psychology into a remarkable accounting of our world in *Thought, Choice, Action*. He gracefully tackles existential questions from a Christian perspective, providing an inspirational analysis of modern issues through his personable literary style. This book explores the meaning of how we choose to live in this world. It offers the reader a consummate literary and spiritual examination of human thought and behavior across the centuries, and delivers an inducive call to active faith.

~ Dr. Ryan Blackstock, Michigan School for Professional Psychology

While exploring the vexing problem of evil in the world and ourselves by drawing on St. Augustine's tripolarity theory that human agents, the divine and the contra-divine can be authentically accounted for within the bounds of Biblical revelation, Sandison's contribution is not that he goes intellectually beyond Augustine's theory much less solve evil's inscrutability, but that he offers to a modern reader, be-deviled by personal tragedy and injustice, the opportunity to discover the healing which he, and many others whose stories he tells, have experienced. Sandison's work belongs to the genre of pastoral theology couched in a context of Biblical theology.

~ Dr. James F. Lewis, Professor of Religious Studies, Bethel University, St. Paul, MN

As part of his long journey to understand and live Truth, Ron Sandison found a welcome place of rest in the works of Augustine. In Augustine, Ron finds the foundation for his concept of the Tripolarity Theory as an explanation for our perceptions of and reactions to events in our lives. *Thought, Choice, Action* offers an overview of this theory as well as an attempt to apply it to real life situations. This book offers readers some fascinating concepts regarding the problem of evil, decision making in a biblical worldview, and free will, and I think it also offers a good launching point for further conversations on the issue of how some of us perceive and respond to reality within a biblical worldview.

~ Dr. Leo Percer, Associate Professor of Biblical Studies, Liberty University Baptist Theological Seminary, Lynchburg, VA

Ron Sandison has written an engaging, scholarly analysis of the human predicament based upon interrelated critical principles employed in the tripolarity theory. He shows how the theory is grounded in Scripture and supported by eminent theologians ancient and modern. The theory advances the three-pronged thesis that each person is created with free will to choose God's goodness over Satan's evil. The strength of the presentation is not the novelty of the theory but the fresh manner in which it is explicated and applied. The clear theological expositions and specific personal applications will nurture the faith of the contemporary Christian reader and hopefully attract the interest of those outside the faith.

~ Dr. Robert Mansfield, Professor of New Testament Emeritus, Graduate School of Theology and Ministry, Oral Roberts University, Tulsa, OK

Ron Sandison's book *Thought, Choice, Action* integrates insights from Scripture, psychology, and Christian theology to address the fundamental human problems of why evil things happen, and how they can be prevented or overcome. Sandison proposes his "Tripolarity Theory" in which human free choice interacts with the demonic and the divine in decision-making. The author applies these insights to life in his own remarkable testimony and other interesting personal stories. This is a good read with excellent insights for Christian decision-making.

~ Dr. Steve Lemke, Provost, Professor of Philosophy and Ethics, New Orleans Baptist Theological Seminary and Editor of the *Journal for Baptist Theology and Ministry*

From its beginnings in the early Church, Christian theology has properly never been an abstract exercise, but pursued with a balance of theory and practice, each informing the other and made substantial in the lives of Christians. Theology is correctly understood as a practical exercise that bears fruit in a manner of life that maintained within a conscious and intelligent relationship with God who grants us salvation in his Son, Jesus Christ. Ron Sandison's book is thus written within this long tradition of theology and, at the same time, is timely and fully addresses the Christian life as it is lived at the heart of our own time and contemporary culture.

~ Dr. David Jasper, Professor of Literature and Theology, University of Glasgow, Scotland and Distinguished Overseas Professor of Religious Studies, Renmin University of China

In loving memory of Debora Ann Clements (1957-2016) who edited the entire manuscript of Thought, Choice, Action, *and her faithful devotion to her family and Christ.*

I have fought the good fight, I have finished the race, I have kept the faith.

2 Timothy 4:7

My beautiful wife, Kristen Sandison, and our daughter, Makayla. For your unconditional love and support.

She brings him good, and not harm, all the days of her life.

Proverbs 31:12

My parents, Chuck & Janet Sandison, for teaching me the Scriptures and helping me overcome my learning disabilities with autism.

Do you see a man skilled in his labor? He will serve before kings; he will not serve before obscure men.

Proverbs 22:29

Foreword
Dr. Ron Rhodes

I HAVE ALWAYS BELIEVED that Bible doctrine is immensely practical. Biblical doctrine enables us to develop a realistic worldview, without which we are doomed to ineffectual living (Matthew 22:23-33; Romans 12:3; 2 Timothy 4:3-4). Moreover, doctrine can protect us from false beliefs that can lead to destructive behavior (1 Timothy 4:1-6; 2 Timothy 2:18; Titus 1:11). Ron Sandison's new book, *Thought, Choice, Action*, is brimming with such practical doctrine.

Sandison's book is satisfying on several levels. It is not only intellectually stimulating, it is also spiritually transforming. It is not just theological, it is also highly applicational.

But—*I know what you're thinking!*—what on earth is the tripolarity theory? Don't let that abstruse term scare you away from the book. The tripolarity theory was formulated by church father and theologian Augustine back in the fifth century. Simply put, the theory says that in every circumstance in life, there are three primary active forces and intelligent agents vying for control and influence: (1) humanity (with our freedom of choice), (2) the devil, and (3) God.

The book demonstrates in a cogent way how both godly and demonic influences can impact our lives on a daily basis. Choosing whom to listen to is all-important, for choices have consequences. Choosing God's will, for example, is a path of blessing, while choosing to heed Satan's voice is a path of despair and defeat. Choosing God's way leads to the life abundant, while choosing the devil's way leads to a life of brokenness. Responding to godly influences leads to goodness and well-being, while responding to demonic influences leads to moral, spiritual, and existential darkness. Understandably, the book ultimately challenges the reader: *Choose this day whom ye shall listen to.*

I was especially interested to see Sandison's discussion of how the theory helped move his life from defeat to victory. By learning and applying the doctrinal points of the tripolarity theory—by choosing to listen to and obey God instead of listening to other voices—he was able to overcome substantial personal challenges relating to both a learning disability and an auditory disability. For Sandison, what *could* have been a life of defeat became a life of victory and overcoming. God's strength became manifest in Sandison's weakness.

Sandison wants to show his readers how the same can be true in each of their lives. Toward this end, he shows how the tripolarity theory relates to many different areas of daily life. By the time the reader finishes the book, he finds that his Christian worldview has been enhanced in a positive way, enabling him to better live the good life as God intended.

One thing worth singling out in the book is Sandison's emphasis on not only *listening* to the voice of God, but also on *choosing to obey* Him. We are called not only to *right belief* but also to *right action*. Christianity is far more than a set of doctrinal propositions. Christianity at its heart involves a personal relationship with Jesus Christ that shows itself in unqualified obedience to His Word.

Sandison recognizes that we go to the pages of Scripture not to merely cram our heads with a bunch of facts but to enlarge our acquaintance on a personal level with God—more particularly, with Jesus Christ—and to learn how to live in a way pleasing to Him. Obedience to God's Word must not be seen as an end in itself. We must seek to learn God's Word and obey it because we treasure our personal relationship and daily walk with God and do not want it to be hindered by foolish choices and actions on our part (Psalm 119:11). I am happy to recommend *Thought, Choice, Action: Decision-*

making that Releases the Holy Spirit's Power, by Ron Sandison. You will be blessed in both mind and heart. I pray that the book finds a wide audience.

Dr. Ron Rhodes, President of Reasoning from the Scriptures Ministries, author of over 60 books (including 3 Silver Medallion winners and the Harvest Gold Award for over a million Harvest House books sold)

CONTENTS

Foreword by Dr. Ron Rhodes vii

Introduction 1

    Why the Tripolarity Theory? 2

    St. Augustine & the Tripolarity Theory.....................................3

    Perspective..3

    Interpretation 5

    Experience God 6

Chapter 1—Power of the Holy Spirit 7

    Introduction...7

    Greater Works...9

    Heaven's Down Payment...10

    Empowerment 11

    The Gift of the Holy Spirit...12

    Being Led by the Holy Spirit..14

    Two Wolves..15

    Sensitive to the Holy Spirit 15

    Jaded Hearts..17

    Supernatural Power 18

    Summary 18

Chapter 2—Hidden God..19

    Introduction...19

    Miracle on the Hudson 20

    External Control..21

    Equipped for a Miracle 22

    Evacuation 23

External or Internal 23

One Year Anniversary 24

Impact & Perspective 24

Faith to See 25

Miracles & Devotion 25

Catastrophe on the Potomac River 26

God's Presence 27

The Tripolarity 27

Internal locus & Inexperience 27

The Devil...28

God's Care 28

Condition of the Heart..29

Presuppositions 29

Miracles Require Faith 30

Ever-present Help 30

Trust 31

Summary 31

Chapter 3—Love of God **33**

Introduction...33

Meaning of Love..34

Transforming Love..35

Woman at the Well...35

Whole-hearted Commitment 38

Complete Devotion 38

Perverted Love...39

Two Masters 39

Hardened Heart...40

Led Astray 41

Love God & Be Free 42

Summary 42

Chapter 4—Origin of the Devil **43**

Introduction...44

The Devil's Origin 44

Rebellion 46

Devil's Fall 48

Grace..50

Christ's Blood...50

Deception..51

Devil's Lie 52

Spiritual Warfare 52

Resist the Devil 53

Summary 54

**Chapter 5—Insidious Operation of the Devil:
Part 1 (Judas Iscariot)..55**

Introduction..55

Judas' Betrayal 56

Judas' Choice..58

The Zealots 59

Judas' Disobedience 60

Judas' Heart...62

Insidious Traps 62

Silent Intruders 63

Light & Darkness..63

Fulfillment of Scriptures......................................64

Worldly Sorrow 65

Divine Irony 65

Consequences..66

Summary 67

**Chapter 6—Insidious Operation of the Devil:
Part 2 (Atheist Madalyn O'Hair) 69**

Introduction..69

The Flaw of Atheism...70

Hell of Violence 70

Natural Born Killer...71

Criminal Mind 72

Road to Perdition...72

First Blood 73

Killer on Parole 74

Demonic Connection..74

Tragic Demise 75

Perfect Crime...76

Hidden Wealth...77

Disappearance..78

Held Captive by the Beasts 78

Unsolved Mystery 79

Connecting the Dots...80

The Final Piece of the Puzzle 81

God's Agents...82

The Devil..82

Choice...82

God 83

Summary 83

Chapter 7—Perception and Choice...............................85

Introduction...85

Perception & Choice...87

Perverted..89

Ananias & Sapphira 94

Perception & Choice...96

Perception & People...97

Angels 98

Destiny 98

Summary 99

Chapter 8—Growth 101

Introduction...102

Source of Growth...102

Fruitfulness..103

New Heart 103

Renewing Our Minds 104

Mindsets 105

Types of Growth 107

Spiritual Growth 108

Devil's Tool 108

The Process of Change 110

Appetite 111

Growth & Loci of Control 112

Hindrance of Growth 113

Choice & Motivation 113

Summary 114

Chapter 9—Creation **115**

Introduction 115

God's Goodness 116

Nature & the Bible 118

Divine Virtues 119

Types of Revelation 120

Special Revelation 120

Trinity 121

Presuppositions 122

Atheists' Presuppositions 123

Theodicy 126

Free Will 127

The Devil 128

Redemption 128

Summary 130

Chapter 10—The Fall **131**

Introduction 131

Present Crisis 132

Paradise Lost 133

Downward Spiral 134

General & Specific 137

Response 138

Book of Job 139

Tempter 140

Job's Response 140

Round Two 140

Job's Friends 141

Message of Job 141

Our Response 143

Summary 143

Chapter 11—Incarnation 145

Introduction 145

Ministry of Jesus 146

Seven Jewish Feasts 146

Year of Jubilee 148

The Birth of Jesus 148

King 149

Priest 149

Atonement Sacrifice 149

Temptation of Christ 149

Power of the Kingdom 150

Divine Nature 151

Worshipped 151

Trinity 151

Diabolic Counterfeit 152

Antichrist's Appearing 154

Tripolarity Theory 155

Christ's Lordship 155

Summary 156

Chapter 12—Eschatology 157

Introduction 157

Second Coming 158

Eschatology 160
Day & Hour Unknown 160
Prepared..161
Christ's Return 161
Last Days 163
Delay in the παρουσια................................163
The Battle 164
Now & Not Yet 165
Prepare the Way of the Lord........................166
Free Will..168
Summary 170

Endnotes **171**
Introduction..171
Holy Spirit 172
Hidden God..172
Love of God 173
Origin of the Devil.....................................173
Insidious Operation of the Devil: Part 1.............173
Insidious Operation of the Devil: Part 2.............174
Perception and Choice 174
Growth 175
Creation..175
The Fall..175
Incarnation..176
Eschatology 176

Bibliography **177**

Articles **183**

Introduction

We have examined this, and it is true.
So hear it and apply it to yourself

Job 5:27

We may not know the exact causation for our circumstances and situations but with the tripolarity theory we can determine our proper response and attitude to overcome.

Ron Sandison

ONE OF MY FAVORITE CHILDHOOD memories is the times I rode my bike to the corner drugstore, purchased a twenty-five-cent bottle of Faygo or a fifty-cent New York Seltzer, and then proceeded on my journey to the park to catch crayfish. I would bring a jar in my backpack for the river monster catch. At the main spot in the river where I caught crayfish the water was murky and there were many jagged rocks for these creatures to hide.

The best method for catching an 8.5-inch crawdad was to enter the river until the water reached my knees, lean over a rock, wait patiently for the crayfish's claws to appear, and then with one swoop catch it. After the catch, I had to wait five minutes for the sediment to settle before the creature was revealed. It took time to tell if I had a trophy or a miss. Like the crayfish in a jar with murky water, we will not always discern the agents of our circumstances (God, the devil, or human choice), but time and prayer will open our eyes to see God and His redeeming power. Our perspective can be murky so we must learn to discern the Truth.

Why the Tripolarity Theory?

When you went to bed last night and thoughts about the decisions you made began to haunt you, how did you handle that? Maybe you've been puzzled why a child, now a man, got trapped in alcoholism or drug use despite all the good biblical instruction and devotions at home. You probably have other puzzling events that don't seem to have an easy answer. Every one of us if honest has some dark areas in our lives we desire to change, and in questions of doubt regarding our faith, we wish for clarity.

I faced some of those—and others—as a student, as a minister with autism. They put me on a search for answers no one I knew was giving me—until I discovered an approach that increasingly made sense to me. I'm using a term to describe my discovery that may be foreign to you—the tripolarity theory. You do not have to repeat it five times to remember it because I'll use it every so often, but let me give you a simple explanation. The tripolarity theory is the belief that in situations and circumstances there are three primary active forces and intelligent agents responsible for events. These three agents are humanity (freedom of choice); the devil (evil), which can include demons and ambivalent forces; and God (good), including His angels and faithful servants.

Another term you may not be familiar with that will be used throughout this book is locus of control, which simply describes the agents of causation for an event or action. Locus of control can be both external and internal. External locus of control includes fate, God, devil, and unforeseen forces beyond an individual's own control. Internal locus of control includes circumstances individuals have the ability to control and the power to change by their own choices and actions.

We will examine the Miracle on the Hudson River, the lurid murder of atheist Madalyn Murray O'Hair, Judas Iscariot's betrayal of Christ, the origin of the devil, creation, the fall, the Incarnation, and eschatology and their relationship with the tripolarity theory and locus of control. We will learn to view the world with a tripolarity perspective, which can lead to growth and transformation. Some circumstances we have the power to change (internal) and others are beyond our locus of control (external) but we can always respond with faith in God.

St. Augustine & the Tripolarity Theory

The tripolarity theory was formulated in the fifth century by church father St. Augustine of Hippo in *The City of God*.[1] St. Augustine's *The City of God* outlines the history of God and humanity and the cosmic battle between good and evil. The free-will agents that participate in this battle for St. Augustine are humanity, devil (evil), and God (good) and the battlefield, the earth. Growth and maturity for St. Augustine in the tripolarity are both internal and external. Internal locus is choosing the good/pure by freedom of will; external locus is receiving the power to accomplish this from God and His grace.

St. Augustine writes, "There is a love by which we love what should not be loved (lust). And a man hates this love in himself if he loves the love of whatever is good. Both loves can exist in one and the same person. This co-existence is good for a man in that he can, by increasing in himself the love of what is right (pure love from God), decrease his love of what is evil (lust) until his whole life has been transformed to good and brought to perfection."[2]

Perspective

Our presuppositions (worldview) determine our beliefs and concepts of locus of control. The tripolarity theory can help clarify the different views individuals have of events with relationship to loci of control.

An example of this is my friend Steve's condo destroyed by a fire ignited by welders soldering, and the four different perspectives an individual could interpret the causation of the destruction. The theist

---

[1] See endnotes: St. Augustine's theology.
[2] Vernon J. Bourke editor, Saint Augustine: *The City of God* (New York: Image Books Doubleday, 1958), 238.

view (external locus), "I had all old furniture and God said, 'Let there be light,' and bless God, I got all new furniture from the insurance company!" The hyper-spiritual view (external locus), "I had all new furniture and did not have any homeowners' insurance trusting in God; the devil pulled out his Zippo and bang, I lost everything!" The atheist view (internal locus), "Man, I wish those jerk welders would have done the job right; then I would not have lost my home." The agnostic view (unsure locus of control), "I don't know what the heck happened; I came home from a hard day of work and my condo was burned down!"

The insurance companies' legal term "Act of God" for floods, tornadoes, forest fires, earthquakes, mudslides, and other natural disasters outside human control demonstrates that loci of control are both external and internal in nature like the tripolarity theory. Theorists would use the term "Act of God" as both God's divine wrath with judgment and His miracles or divine intervention for His chosen people.

The tripolarity theory would view Steve's condo fire with both internal locus of control and external: the fire was caused by welders soldering (humanity/internal), there is a devil who comes to kill, steal, and destroy (evil/external) (John 10:10), and God (good/external) is able to transform this bad circumstance into good. Paul said, "And we know that in all things God works for the good of those who love him, who have been called according to his purpose" (Romans 8:28).

Joseph had this attitude toward his brothers who sold him into slavery: "Don't be afraid. Am I in the place of God? (locus of control) You intended to harm me (internal locus), but God (external locus) intended it for good to accomplish what is now being done, the saving of many lives (internal locus with the external)" (Gen. 50:19-20). There is a partnership in the tripolarity theory between God and His creation. Some things are the sovereignty of God and others involve humanity's free choice, but God is able to use them all for His glory.

Interpretation

The baroque-style oil painting *Sacred Love Versus Profane Love* by Giovanni Baglione in 1602 demonstrates the tripolarity theory and the cosmic battle between good and evil. The canvas depicts an angel hovering above a human/cupid figure and the devil hiding in the dark shadows. The face of the figure of the devil at the left has been identified as a portrait of artist Michelangelo Merisi da Caravaggio and is a reflection of Giovanni's animosity toward him. This devil symbolizes a satirical condemnation of both Caravaggio's artwork and his moral scruples.[3] It also demonstrates our interpretation of situations; Giovanni was at legal war with Caravaggio so he viewed him as a devil. Now imagine that Caravaggio would have miraculously rescued Giovanni's youngest son from a house fire; no longer would he be the portrait of the devil but the face of an angel. Our presuppositions determine our interpretation of facts and also the manner we view and judge others. Do we see people as sent from God or the devil's henchmen or a waste of our precious time?

We also, in our tests of life, sometimes view our circumstances only from one limited perspective. Some believers in a test say, "Oh, the devil is beating me down!" Another may explain their hardships stating, "My wrong decisions have created these circumstances; I have made my bed and now I am forced to sleep in it!" Still others focus solely on the divine: "God is the One who has placed me in this test to develop my character and make me fit for eternity." These explanations are simplistic and fail to comprehend the complexity of situations or take into account the infinite multivalent factors that affect our lives. A believer who is stable realizes trials are usually complex and caused by different factors and therefore we need to trust God and seek His guidance.

---

[3] See endnotes: Caravaggio's character and reputation.

Experience God

Thought, Choice, Action: Decision-making that Releases the Holy Spirit's Power will teach us how to experience God in our lives, grow spiritually, take responsibility for our decisions, and advance the kingdom of God. This book will not give you just theological ideas and philosophical concepts, but practical insight into the Kingdom of God. Each chapter will examine a different aspect of the tripolarity theory and its impact on our lives.

As we read, the two things we should do are listen to the voice of God and obey Him as we walk in obedience; we will experience a deeper relationship with Christ. When Samuel was called by the Lord, Eli told him to say, "Speak, Lord, for your servant is listening" (1 Sam. 3:9). This needs to be our hearts' cry also: "Speak, Lord, for (put your name here) your servant is listening." After we hear from God we must obey and apply His Word to our lives. Mary instructed the servants at the wedding in which Jesus transformed the water into wine, "Do whatever he (Jesus) tells you" (John 2:5). This faithfulness and obedience enable us to hear God and grow spiritually. John Bevere said, "Revelation is of no value without the wisdom and character to live it out."

The tripolarity theory teaches us that our choices really do matter and sound faith consists of orthodox theology (right beliefs and doctrines) and orthopraxy (the living of the faith—right actions). As we choose to follow Christ (internal locus) and live by His grace (external locus), we see the world from God's perspective.

Father Clement wrote, "For when the pagans hear from our mouths the oracles and promises of God, they marvel at their beauty and greatness. But when they discover that our actions are not worthy of the words we speak, they turn from wonder to blasphemy, saying it is only a myth and delusion" (2 Clement 13:3). May our lives and actions create wonder at the greatness of God and cause people to see Christ in us, the hope of glory.

Chapter 1
Power of the Holy Spirit

Not by might nor by power, but by my Spirit.

Zechariah 4:6

I would like to learn just one thing from you: Did you receive the Spirit by observing the law, or by believing what you heard?

Galatians 3:2

Everything we do in our own strength apart from the Holy Spirit's power is equivalent to painting a barn that is already on fire.

Ron Sandison

I need to be filled daily afresh with the Holy Spirit because like a water faucet I too leak.

D.L. Moody

Introduction

FLAGSTAFF WAS A PRETTY NORMAL small town in Somerset County, Maine. In 1948 Central Maine Power purchased the residents' homes and properties with the help of the government and announced in a year this valley would be flooded to create a reservoir serving hydroelectric dams downstream. This would enhance the river drive delivering timber to the pulp mills and bring new jobs to their region. The following year, the residents in this community ceased to tend their gardens and mow their lawns, or maintain and improve their homes, since in a few months these homes would be submerged under the water of the Flagstaff Lake. If a window broke, the glass was left on the ground unattended. In the days before the flooding the area appeared as a ghost town. A news reporter from the city interviewed a local resident about the condition of the once prosperous valley and the local replied, "Why paint a house that will be flooded in a few days and why make repairs if your town will be destroyed? Where there is no faith in the future, there is no power in the present!"[4]

The Holy Spirit empowers us in the present and creates faith in our hearts. The Apostle Paul wrote, "And hope does not disappoint us, because God has poured out his love into our hearts by the Holy Spirit, whom he has given us" (Rom. 5:5). The community of Flagstaff had no faith for their town's future, since it would be destroyed, and this caused them to take no action in the present. Jesus promised His followers the power of the Holy Spirit. John 16:7 states, "But I tell you the truth: It is for your good that I am going away. Unless I go away, the Counselor will not come to you; but if I go, I will send him to you." The Holy Spirit is Christ's presence in our lives and He empowers us to live for God. Ephesians 2:22 says, "And in him (Christ) you too are being built together to become a dwelling in which God lives by his Spirit."

In the Garden of Eden, God walked with Adam and Eve by the cool of the day (Gen. 3:8). During the exodus God manifested His presence by a cloud by day and a pillar of fire at night (Exodus 13:21-22). In the time of King Solomon, the Lord dwelt in His holy temple in Jerusalem (1 King 8). Through the incarnation God revealed Himself through Jesus Christ His only Son (John 14:7-8; Col. 2:9). In the present time, God dwells in the hearts of His children by the Holy Spirit (1 Cor. 3:16-17, 1 Cor. 6:19-20).

---

[4] See endnotes: Holy Spirit.

Greater Works

When Jesus promised the Holy Spirit to His disciples in John's Gospel, John used the word αλλος meaning another of the exact same nature or kind to demonstrate the Holy Spirit's presence in the believers is the same as having Jesus physically present. Jesus said, "And I will ask the Father, and he will give you another Counselor to be with you forever." J. Dwight Pentecost from Dallas Theological said, "In Jesus' absence He would send them 'another' Helper. The Greek word for 'another' infers 'another just like Myself.' The Holy Spirit would do for the disciples all that Christ had done for them while He was with them."[5]

The incarnation limited Jesus' presence on earth to only one location; Christ was hindered from being in both Jerusalem and Judah simultaneously by His physical body. Jesus in His earthly ministry was unable to heal a multitude in Samaria and at the same time lay hands on a person in Jerusalem since in the incarnation He was unable to be in two places at once.

The Holy Spirit is the Spirit of God and is not limited by space and time. A woman in Africa can pray for healing and simultaneously a businessman in Japan, and both can receive the answer to their urgent request. As John 3:34 states, "The Spirit is given without limit or without measure."

Jesus said, "I tell you the truth, anyone who has faith in me will do what I have been doing. He will do even greater things than these, because I am going to the Father" (John 14:12). The disciples and believers will do even greater (μειζονα) works because the Holy Spirit is present in all Christ's followers and empowers them for ministry.

---

[5] J. Dwight Pentecost, *The Words & Works of Jesus Christ* (Grand Rapids: Zondervan, 1981), 438.

Heaven's Down Payment

The Apostle Paul wrote, "Set his seal of ownership on us, and puts his Spirit in our hearts as a deposit, guaranteeing what is to come" (2 Cor. 1:22). 2 Corinthians 5:5 says, "Now it is God who has made us for this very purpose and has given us the Spirit as a deposit, guaranteeing what is to come." In these two verses, Paul uses the Greek word αρραβων which means a deposit, pledge, earnest and down payment. The term means a deposit which is in itself a guarantee that the full amount will be paid.[6] Through the Holy Spirit and His working in our lives we receive the blessings and provision of God. The deposit of the Spirit, God's down payment, guarantees at Christ's return we will receive the fullness of His promises.

Jesus' prayer in the Sermon on the Mount states, "Your kingdom come, your will be done on earth as it is in heaven" (Matt. 6:10). When we receive a miracle from heaven, like a healing it is αρραβων "down payment," reminding us at Christ's return we are guaranteed to have perfect physical health and no sickness. Matthew 12:28 states, "But if I drive out demons by the Spirit of God, then the kingdom of God has come to you." Professor Jeffrey Burton Russell wrote, "Each act of exorcism represented one installment of the destruction of the old age, one step closer to the time when Satan will no longer control the world."[7]

When we receive financial blessings it is also αρραβων "down payment," the pavement in heaven, reminding us of our guaranteed home in paradise where the streets are gold (Rev. 21:18). These αρραβων blessings remind us at Christ's return creation will once again be restored. Acts 3:21 says, "Jesus must remain in heaven until the time comes for God to restore everything, as he promised through his holy prophets."

---

[6] Cleon Rogers, Jr. and Cleon Rogers, III. *The New Linguistic Key to the Greek New Testament* (Grand Rapids: Zondervan, 1998), 394.

[7] Jeffrey Burton Russell, *The Prince of Darkness* (Ithaca and London: Cornell University Press, 1988), 47.

Revelation 21:4 describes this paradisiacal condition: "God will wipe every tear from their eyes. There will be no more death or mourning or crying or pain, for the old order of things has passed away." The Holy Spirit is the deposit and guarantees we as God's children will inherit the new heaven and new earth.

The Holy Spirit reveals the spiritual realm. 1 Corinthians 2:12 states, "We have not received the spirit of the world but the Spirit who is from God, that we may understand what God has freely given us."

The unbeliever or skeptic, when they examine our miracle testimonies of healing, God's intervention, or financial blessings may mock, "You were just lucky" or "That form of cancer is curable." Our presuppositions determine whether we are able to see God's miracles or we choose to explain them away by natural processes. The Apostle Paul said, "The man without the Spirit does not accept the things that come from the Spirit of God, for they are foolishness to him, and he cannot understand them, because they are spiritually discerned" (1 Cor. 2:14).

Empowerment

1 Samuel 10:6-7 says, "The Spirit of the Lord will come upon you in power (external locus) and you will prophesy with them; and you will be changed into a different person. Once these signs are fulfilled, do whatever your hand (internal locus) finds to do, for God is with you." The Spirit of the Lord empowered King Saul to prophesy and be changed into a man of faith and courage. This empowerment would have enabled King Saul to use his natural gifts to serve God.

Instead of following the Spirit, King Saul with a proud heart and fear of men disobeyed God and the Prophet Samuel. King Saul had grown impatient as he waited for the Prophet Samuel and decided to make the offerings to the Lord himself. Samuel commanded King Saul, "You must wait seven days until I come to you and tell you what you are to do" (1 Samuel 10:8). The burnt offering was to be performed by a priest or prophet and not a king. When Samuel arrived King Saul told him, "I felt compelled to offer the burnt offerings" (1 Sam. 13:12). Samuel rebuked Saul for his disobedience and pronounced the judgment his kingdom would not endure.

Unlike Saul the Prophet Samuel waited upon the Lord. When the Lord spoke to Samuel, he replied, "Speak, for your servant is listening" (1 Sam. 3:10). Samuel's obedience resulted in his receiving deep revelation and having authority as a prophet. A.W. Tozer said, "The Holy Spirit will sharpen the arrows of the man or woman of God who preaches the whole counsel of God." 1 Samuel 3:19-21 says,

> "The Lord was with Samuel as he grew up, and he let none of his words fall to the ground. And all Israel from Dan to Beersheba recognized that Samuel was attested as a prophet of the Lord. The Lord continued to appear at Shiloh, and there he revealed himself to Samuel through his word. And Samuel's word came to all Israel."

The Gift of the Holy Spirit

Jesus told His followers before He ascended back to heaven, "Do not leave Jerusalem, but wait for the gift my Father promised, which you have heard me speak about. For John baptized with water, but in a few days you will be baptized with the Holy Spirit" (Acts 1:4-5). The number of disciples waiting for the promise in Jerusalem had dwindled from five hundred to only one hundred and twenty on the Day of Pentecost (Acts 1:15, 1 Cor. 15:6). This faithful remnant of one hundred and twenty would be filled with the Holy Spirit and receive God's power (Acts 2:1-13). The Apostle Peter preached, "We are witnesses of these things, and so is the Holy Spirit, whom God has given to those who obey him" (Acts 5:32).

We like King Saul have a choice to either allow the Holy Spirit to lead us or to follow our own impulsive desires. If we choose to let the Spirit lead us then He will transform us into a new person. The Apostle Paul wrote, "And we, who with unveiled faces all reflect the Lord's glory, are being transformed into his likeness with ever-increasing glory, which comes from the Lord, who is the Spirit" (2 Cor. 3:18).

That's why the Scriptures command us, "Not to grieve the Holy Spirit of God, with whom you were sealed for the day of redemption" and "Do not put out the Spirit's fire" (Eph. 4:30, 1 Thess. 5:19). These rebellious attitudes hinder us from being transformed into Christ's image and operating in the Spirit's power. As we live by the Holy Spirit, He fills us with His presence. Ephesians 5:18 says, "Do not get drunk on wine which leads to debauchery. Instead, be filled with the Spirit."

The Holy Spirit influences us to make right decisions and He convicts us of our sins and their consequences. The Apostle Paul wrote, "So I say, live by the Spirit, and you will not gratify the desires of the sinful nature (flesh). For the sinful nature desires what is contrary to the Spirit, and the Spirit what is contrary to the sinful nature. They are in conflict with each other, so that you do not do what you want. But if you are led by the Spirit you are not under law" (Gal. 5:16-18).

The flesh or sinful nature influences us to rebel against God and do the devil's work. Galatians 5:19-21 describes this demonic influence: "The acts of the sinful nature are obvious: sexual immorality, impurity and debauchery; idolatry and witchcraft; hatred, discord, jealousy, fits of rage, selfish ambitions, dissensions, factions, and envy; drunkenness, orgies, and the like. I warned you, as I did before, that those who live like this will not inherit the kingdom of God." We have a choice (human agent) to be like King Saul and follow the flesh; i.e., the sinful nature or the Spirit. The Spirit brings life and the sinful nature death.

In chapter seven of Romans, the Apostle Paul humbly confessed his inability by his own strength to obey God's law and declared, "For what I want to do I do not do, but what I hate I do" and "What a wretched man I am" (Rom. 7:15; 7:24). Paul realized that apart from the Holy Spirit's power he was unable to live a life that pleased God.

Being Led by the Holy Spirit

How do we live by the Spirit so we don't fulfill the desires of the flesh? **First**, for us to live by the Spirit, we must be born again and receive Him (John 3). Jesus said, "If you then, though you are evil, know how to give good gifts to your children how much more will your Father in heaven give the Holy Spirit to those who ask him" (Luke 11:13). As children of God the Holy Spirit lives in us and guides our paths.

Second, we should remember that as children of God, we have a choice to either live by the flesh or the Spirit. As we live by the Spirit the sinful nature loses its grip on our minds and lives. The Holy Spirit transforms our desires into the desires of God and we cease to have an appetite to feed the sinful nature. Our thoughts become pure and we begin to see the world from God's perspective with a desire to help those around us.

As a house may have many different rooms—the kitchen, bedrooms, restrooms, walk-in closet, and a cellar—the Holy Spirit leads us to clean the areas of our lives like spring-cleaning of a house. He convicts us to pick up the dirty clothes in our bedroom of lust and greed, or the walk-in closet filled with hidden addictions. We have a choice to follow the Spirit's leading or ignore His conviction. Being led by the Spirit is simply allowing the Spirit to work and reign over our lives.

Living by the flesh is not allowing the Holy Spirit to have His influence over our lives. Maybe we allow the Spirit to clean the bedrooms, kitchen, and living-room but keep a deadbolt lock on the dark cellar filled with porn or greed. In the area of relationships, this personal decision to lock the cellar of our heart will cause us to be led by our lustful passions rather than the Spirit.

Third, we bear fruit by the Holy Spirit's influence in our lives. Galatians 5:22-23 says, "But the fruit of the Spirit is love, joy, peace, patience, kindness, goodness, faithfulness, gentleness and self-control. Against such things there is no law." The degree to which we are submitted to God and allow His Spirit to lead us determines our ability to produce fruit.

Two Wolves

If we crucify the desire of the sinful nature by not allowing it to have influence in our lives we will be led by the Spirit. If we feed the appetites of our flesh and choose to ignore the Holy Spirit's conviction our flesh will dominate. A ranger had two beautiful wolves on a chain. The first wolf was a pure white color and the other a dirty gray. The ranger asked a group of spectators, "Which of these two wolves would win in a fight to the death?" A child raised his hand and said, "The white wolf!" The ranger replied, "The wolf that survives will be the one that is fed and cared for. If I feed the gray wolf and starve the white, the gray will be victorious. But if the gray wolf is starved and the white one is fed and trained, the white will prevail!" In the same way, for us to live by the Spirit, we need to put to death the desires of the flesh.

Sensitive to the Holy Spirit

Sensory adaptation occurs when our sensory receptors change their sensitivity to stimulus. This phenomenon occurs in all our senses with the only exception being the sense of pain. Sensory adaptation causes a repetitive loud noise signal to fade. During spring break Logan, whose room was right next to mine, forgot to disconnect his alarm clock and every morning at 6:00 a.m. his radio played deafening heavy metal rock music which lasted four hours. The first two days I could barely think because the music was so deafening; I kept fantasizing smashing his alarm clock with a sledge hammer. By the third day, a miracle occurred; I ceased to be distracted by the sound because my ears had blocked the sensation of the music.

As our sense of perception can be dulled through sensory adaptation, so disobedience can dull our sensitivity to the Holy Spirit. Disobedience causes our hearts to become hardened toward God and the tender voice of the Holy Spirit.

When this occurs God sometimes uses discipline as a means to lead His children back to His heart. C.S Lewis writes, "We can rest contentedly in our sins and in our stupidities; and anyone who has watched gluttons shoveling down the most exquisite foods as if they did not know what they were eating will admit that we can ignore even pleasure. But pain insists upon being attended to. God whispers to us in our pleasures, speaks in our conscience, but shouts in our pain: it is His megaphone to rouse a deaf world."[8]

God's discipline is the absence of the sense of His tangible presence and provision in our lives that cause us to turn in repentance to Him. 2 Chronicles 7:14 describes this process of repentance as it relates to the nation of Israel: "If my people, who are called by my name, will humble themselves and pray and seek my face and turn from their wicked ways, then will I hear from heaven and will forgive their sin and will heal their land." The parody *Butt-prints in the Sand* humorously describes the conditions for our receiving divine discipline.

Butt-prints in the Sand

One night I had a wondrous dream,
One set of footprints there was seen,
The footprints of my precious Lord,
But mine were not along the shore.

But then some stranger prints appeared,
And I asked the Lord, "What have we here?"
Those prints are large and round and neat,
"But Lord they are too big for feet."

"My child," He said in somber tones,
"For miles I carried you alone.

---

[8] C.S Lewis, *The Problem of Pain* (New York: Macmillan Pub. 1962), 93.

I challenged you to walk in faith,
But you refused and made me wait."

"You disobeyed, you would not grow,
The walk of faith, you would not know.
So I got tired, I got fed up,
and there I dropped you on your butt."

"Because in life, there comes a time,
when one must fight, and one must climb.
When one must rise and take a stand,
or leave their butt-prints in the sand."[9]

Jaded Hearts

John 12:28-30 says, "Father, glorify your name! Then came a voice from heaven, 'I have glorified it, and will glorify it again.' The crowd that was there and heard it said it had thundered; others said an angel had spoken to him. Jesus said, 'This voice was for your benefit, not mine.'" The people's hearts were jaded and this caused them to perceive the voice of God as muffled or thunder and they were unable to comprehend Jesus' true identity as the Son of God.

We break free from jadedness by renewing our hearts and minds through the word of God. Romans 12:2 states, "Do not conform any longer to the pattern of this world, but be transformed by the renewing of your mind. Then you will be able to test and approve what God's will is—his good, pleasing and perfect will." As we read the Scriptures, the Holy Spirit teaches us to apply God's word to our lives; He causes certain verses to speak directly to our situations. Jesus said, "But the Counselor, the Holy Spirit, whom the Father will send in my name, will teach you all things and will remind you of everything I have said to you" (John 14:26).

---

[9] Author unknown

Supernatural Power

King David sang, "With your help I can advance against a troop; with my God I can scale a wall, or run through a barricade" (Psalm 18:29). Oral Roberts preached, "God wants to do the impossible through me who it is impossible to do it through." As we are led by the Holy Spirit, we receive supernatural power to accomplish God's work. The Holy Spirit gives the strength to follow Christ daily and do the impossible. In the movie *Superman*, Lois Lane was only able to fly as she clung to Superman. As soon as her hands drifted even little from his grasp, Lois began to free-fall to the earth. We also must depend on the Holy Spirit to guide our lives. Like a hang glider needs the wind's breeze to compel it to higher heights so we depend on the Spirit for our strength.

Summary

The Holy Spirit in the tripolarity theory is our source of power to live godly lives. The devil attempts to lead us astray through disobedience. We have a choice to live by the Holy Spirit which leads to life or the flesh that leads to death. The Apostle Paul summarizes it best: "Do not be deceived: God cannot be mocked. A man reaps what he sows. The one who sows to please his sinful nature, from that nature will reap destruction; the one who sows to please the Spirit, from the Spirit will reap eternal life. Let us not become weary in doing good, for at the proper time we will reap a harvest if we do not give up" (Gal. 6:7-9).

Chapter 2
Hidden God

Miracles are a retelling in small letters of the very same story which is written across the whole world in letters too large for some of us to see.

C.S. Lewis

Miracles are not contrary to nature, but contrary to what we know about nature.

St. Augustine

Truly you are a God who hides himself, O God and Savior of Israel.

Isaiah 45:15

We live by faith, not by sight.

2 Corinthians 5:7

Introduction

I WAS RAISED IN A denomination which taught the providence of God but did not stress the importance of miracles for today. When I received a scholarship to Oral Roberts University founded by a healing minister, I began to question the concept of miracles. In the center of the ORU basketball court at the Mabee Center is written, "Expect a Miracle." As I read this, I used to think, "If God is all-powerful and able to perform wonders, why at times does it feel like He is absent?" While in college, many nights, I struggled with these thoughts about the character of God and His providence.

When your loved one dies unexpectedly or a close friend of yours receives the report the cancer has returned, how do you discover the power to move forward and the grace to see the presence of God? A biblically sound understanding of miracles and catastrophe based on the tripolarity theory can help us deal with these questions.

Miracle on the Hudson

On January 15, 2009, at 3:27 p.m., US Airways Flight 1549 Captain Chesley "Sully" Sullenberger reported a "double bird strike." A flock of twelve-pound Canada geese struck Flight 1549 shortly after takeoff as the aircraft was reaching speeds of 150 mph. The force of impact was equivalent to a 1,000-pound weight being dropped from 10 feet. The "bird strike" force caused both engines to be inoperable. The cool-headed Captain Sully maneuvered his 160,000-pound jetliner over New York City and managed to land the A320 jet in the frigid Hudson River. All one hundred fifty passengers plus the five crew members on board were evacuated onto the wings and the inflatable slides and then were taken by ferries safely to the harbor.

Amazingly, only one passenger suffered serious injuries; a woman had two broken legs. Governor David Peterson coined the landing, "A miracle on the Hudson!" Governor Peterson said, "We had a miracle on 34th Street. I believe now we have had a miracle on the Hudson." Passenger Joe Hart said, "Both engines cut out and Captain Sully actually floated it into the river. It was like the hand of God!" Eyewitness Gloria Shafter said, "I saw this plane coming down and all that I could think was, are all these people going to tragically die? Or will there be a miracle? It was like watching 9/11 all over again!" [10]

Truly, this event appeared to be a miracle similar to when the Israelites crossed the Red Sea, when the walls of Jericho fell after the Israelites' victory march, or when Jesus turned water into wine.

---

[10] See endnotes: St. Augustine's definition of a miracle.

Even the odds of the landing seem to indicate a miracle on the Hudson River; it was beyond human comprehension. Paul says, "Oh, the depth of the riches of the wisdom and knowledge of God! How unsearchable his judgments, and his paths beyond tracing!" (Romans 11:33). Normally, when an aircraft crashes the aftermath includes tragedy and death.

External Control

The "miracle on the Hudson River" required three variables of external loci of control. The Canada geese, the culprit locus, caused the engine failure and inevitable crash. The perfect 36-degree Fahrenheit temperature of the river made the conditions possible to choreograph the crisis landing on water. Finally, the bull's-eye landing was exacted on the vacant river terminal which normally is congested with ferries and cargo ships.

First, for this event to occur, you need the natural force of a flying 1,000-pound projectile (bird strike). Richard Dolbeer in his study states, "Worldwide since 1960, there have been 25 aircraft crashes caused by bird strikes and of these incidents 23 of 25 occurred below 400 feet." The Federal Aviation Administration states, "There were approximately about 65,000 bird strikes to civil aircraft in the U.S. from 1990-2005, or about one for every 10,000 fights. Of these incidences it has been estimated there is only about one accident resulting in human death in one billion flying hours."

The **second** external locus was the frigid temperature of the Hudson River (30-40 degrees Fahrenheit) and the heroic effort of the rescuers with a very limited time frame. Captain Vince Lombardi of the NY Water Co. said, "My crew and commuters helped pull 56 people into our commercial ferry and they even gave the passengers their own coats and shirts off their backs to keep them warm!" Juan Rosario, another Waterway ferry captain, said, "When I saw it I was in shock, but immediately we just sprang into action. We saw it going down slowly, almost like it was descending nicely. There was a big splash! And we immediately changed our course to aid the rescue efforts."

Detective Michael Delany, from the NYPD scuba team, said, "Time was crucial as the passengers struggled in the icy conditions. They were frozen, very lethargic, almost to the point of hypothermia. The water was around 55-65 feet deep, and at its coldest point around 30 degrees Fahrenheit. Plus you have the cold wind, the tide and the -7 Celsius weather. People would have only been able to survive for around 5 to 10 minutes." Captain Rosario also commented on the rescue conditions, "I was surprised and amazed that everyone survived; I assumed people wouldn't survive the freezing water!"

The **third** external locus was Captain Sully's perfect landing and his flight crew's immediate response and orderly evacuation. The plane struck the water a stone's throw from the densely populated avenues of Manhattan, and could have easily hit a building if not for the miracle landing. Flight 1549 was airborne for about three minutes, attaining an altitude of 3,000 feet, before its rapid descent. The aircraft, with its high speed, miraculously was not torn into pieces upon impact; the water density caused by its temperature likely prevented the dreaded cartwheel landing effect. The pilot landed the plane on one of the busiest parts of the river without colliding with any ships. These favorable elements were the external loci of control.

Equipped for a Miracle

Captain Sully's forty-plus years of professional flying experience in addition to his two master's degrees helped equip him for the miraculous landing. Sully's wife, Lorrie Sullenberger, describes her husband as, "The consummate pilot; he is about performing that airplane to the exact precision to which it was made." Gordon MacDonald reflects, "Airline Captain Sully (age 57) has spent his professional life becoming an expert in safety. He is a glider pilot, a military pilot, and an airline pilot. It looks like there could hardly have been a more equipped person at the controls. In the impenetrable mysteries of a providential God, does He nudge a man prepared like this into the pilot's seat for that exact flight? It's worth pondering!"[11]

Exodus 4:17 says, "Take this staff in your hand (internal locus) so that you can perform miraculous signs with it" (external locus). The staff (training) with the power of God equals miracles.

Captain Sully said in an interview on CBS that his training prompted him to choose a ditching location near operating boats so as to maximize the chance of rescue. The location was near three boat terminals; two used by ferry operators and a third by a tour boat operator, all of whom helped in the rescue.

Evacuation

Immediately after the A320 had been ditched, the aircrew began to evacuate the passengers as the water quickly poured in. Flight attendants urged the passengers to move forward by climbing over seats in order to escape the rising water. Even as the water began to fill the cabin, Captain Sully walked calmly down the full length of the plane twice before leaving in order to make sure that everyone had safely evacuated.

External or Internal

Some aviation experts calculate the odds of the miracle on the Hudson's safe landing to be 1 in 900 trillion; about the same odds of Joan Ginther, who won the Texas lottery four times. Our facts and statistics are the hired servants of our presuppositions. Was the miracle on the Hudson an external locus of control (God, luck, fate or destiny), or internal locus of control (the pilot's skills and experience, the aircrew's ability to stay calm under pressure, the rescuers' quick response time, and the passengers' desire to survive), or do we view it like the tripolarity theory as both?

Passenger Alberto Panero exclaimed, "Wow, thank the Lord (external locus) and thank the pilot (internal locus). I still cannot

---

[11] Jan 16, 2009. Newsletter: Miracle on the Hudson by Gordon MacDonald.

believe he managed to land this plane safely. This was a near-death experience and has changed my life forever!" Mike Nunn, who sat by the window overlooking one of the wings, said, "It's a miracle that one of us survived, but that we all survived is something way more than words can express! Almost everyone on the plane believed this was divine intervention except for Captain Sully, but God is not yet finished with him."[12]

One Year Anniversary

A year after the miracle on the Hudson Landing, an anniversary reunion was held for the passengers, crew, and rescuers of Flight 1549. Cheering with joy, they raised their glasses of champagne at 3:31 p.m., the moment of impact, on one of the ferries that plucked their shivering bodies from the icy water just minutes after they had splashed down. The landing also had some other miracle gifts. Karin Hill became Karin Rooney after she married her boyfriend, who was sitting next to her on the flight. Ben Bostic and Laura Zych, strangers at the time of the crash, began dating and have fallen in love, and passenger Jennifer Doyle became pregnant. However, other passengers, including Ann Oblak, have experienced post-traumatic stress disorder from the crash and are now terrified to fly.

Impact & Perspective

For some, the crash created a sense of togetherness. Passenger Vallie Collins said, "We're a family! There's some connection I have with these people that's kind of impossible to explain." Captain Sully wrote a book titled *Highest Duty*. The book describes his professional training, the aircrew, the rescuers, and a little natural luck helped save the 155 people aboard (internal locus). Captain Sully wrote, "There were a dozen different days that I could have died during my

---

[12] Sep. 24, 2010. Article: More Than A Miracle: Hudson plane crash survivor: 'God has a purpose for us' by Phil Sarata

military years. I survived in part because I was a diligent pilot with good judgment, but also because circumstances were with me."[13]

Passenger Frederick Berretta also wrote a book titled *Flight of Faith*. Frederick's book testifies that God miraculously saved his life and those on Flight 1549 with the help of Captain Sully. He attributes that event to be the crystallizing moment for his Christian faith (external locus).

C.S. Lewis said, "God is present enough so that those who want a relationship with Him can and they can know that He is real and cares. And just absent enough so that those who don't want anything to do with Him aren't forced to! Love requires both evidence and hiddenness." Our perception of locus of controls determines if we, like Captain Sully, an atheist (internal locus), believe the landing was skills and training mixed with natural luck or, like passengers Mike Nunn, Alberto Panero, Frederick Berretta, and many others on Flight 1549 as well as the rescuers, believe it was the hand of God with human help (external locus).

Faith to See

Faith and trust give us the ability to see God in the shadow lands of doubt and confusion. Martin Luther, the great Reformer, said, "Faith is a living trust in God's grace." Blaise Pascal, a sixteenth-century French Christian philosopher, said, "God gives enough light to enlighten the elect and enough darkness to blind the reprobate." The choice between doubt and faith depends on our presuppositions and beliefs concerning locus of control.

Miracles & Devotion

G.K Chesterton said, "The worst moment for the atheist is when he is really thankful and has no one to thank."[14] For Captain Sully, his

---

[13] Chesley "Sully" Sullenberger with Jeffrey Zaslow, *Highest Duty* (New York: HarperCollins 2009), 130.

[14] Atheist Madalyn Murray O'Hair, who took prayer from public school; when her charges for resisting arrest were dismissed stated, "Thank God!" This is an

training and natural luck offers no one to praise for the miracle but himself, the rescuers, and his crew. In the tripolarity theory Satan blinds the unbelievers from seeing God's glory of providence in creation. 2 Corinthians 4:4 states, "The god of this age has blinded the minds of unbelievers, so that they cannot see the light of the gospel of the glory of Christ who is the image of God."

Søren Kierkegaard wrote, "A king's existence is demonstrated by way of subjection and submissiveness. Do you want to try and demonstrate that the king exists? Will you do so by offering a string of proofs, a series of arguments? No. If you are serious, you will demonstrate the king's existence by your submission, by the way you live. And so it is with demonstrating God's existence. It is accomplished not by proofs but worship. Any other way is but a thinker's pious bungling."[15]

Catastrophe on the Potomac River

The miracle on the Hudson occurred almost exactly twenty-seven years after Air Florida Flight 90 bound for Tampa crashed into the Potomac River. The crash occurred just after takeoff from Washington National Airport in which 70 passengers and 4 crew members died and only 5 aboard survived.[16] Four motorists on the 14th Street Bridge, which was stuck by the plane, were also killed. The pilots failed to switch on the engines' internal ice protection systems; they used reverse thrust in a snowstorm prior to takeoff, and failed to abort the takeoff even after detecting a power problem with the wing. One of two questions then arises: "Why did those 78 have to die?" or "Why were those 5 spared of the 78?"

---

example of Anselm Theory even an atheist subconsciously believes in God, but yet denies His existence from their conscious mind.

[15] Charles E. Moore, editor, *Provocations Spiritual Writings of Kierkegaard* (Farmington PA: The Plough Publishing House, 2002), 76.

[16] Flight 90 crashed Jan. 13, 1982.

God's Presence

The gracious landing on the Hudson River seemed to be the hand of God, but how do we see God's presence in the catastrophe on the Potomac River with the tragic death of so many? Christian writer Philip Yancey gives us a clue: "A better question to 'Where is God when it hurts?' would be, 'Where is the body of believers?' because if believers are present and they care for those who suffer, God's presence is also visible.'"[17]

The Tripolarity

The tripolarity theory views the crash of Flight 90 with three agents involved: human choice, the devil, and God. Human agents and their choices (free will) were involved. Captain Sully (age 57) and First Officer Jeffrey Skiles (age 49) had forty-plus years' experience. Captain Larry Wheaton (age 34) and First Officer Roger Pettit (age 31) were two young pilots who had only four years' flight experience combined. This lack of experience was demonstrated by Captain Wheaton's decision for takeoff despite ice on the engine and problems with the wing.

Internal locus & Inexperience

First Officer Roger Pettit warned Captain Wheaton of the ice on the wing three times, but his lack of self-confidence, leadership, and communication skills caused him to minimize the problems. As writer Malcolm Gladwell says, "First Officer Pettit communicated with mitigated speech instead of a direct imperative command of urgency." Mitigated speech is an attempt to downplay or sugarcoat the meaning of what is being said. People mitigate when they're trying to be polite, or when ashamed or embarrassed, or in the case of First Officer Pettit being deferential to authority.[18]

---

[17] Philip Yancey, *Where Is God When It Hurts?* (Grand Rapids: Zondervan, 1990), 243.

[18] Malcolm Gladwell, *Outliers* (New York: Brown And Company, 2008), 194.

Read carefully First Officer Pettit's dialogue with Captain Wheaton before the catastrophe as recorded on the black box. (**1ˢᵗ warning**) First Officer: "Look how the ice is just hanging on his, ah, back, back, there, see that?" (**2ⁿᵈ warning**) First Officer: "Boy, this is a, this is a losing battle here on trying to de-ice those things, it (gives) you a false feeling of security, that's all that does." After Flight 90 received clearance for takeoff, First Officer gives a **3ʳᵈ** and final **warning**: "Let's check those (wings) tops again, since we've been setting here awhile." Captain Wheaton responded to First Officer Pettit's mitigated speech: "I think we get to go here in a minute!" Instead of taking heed, Captain Wheaton totally ignored his First Officer's warning.

This dialogue between Captain Wheaton and First Officer Pettit demonstrated their lack of communication and synergy. Captain Sully and First Officer Skiles along with the aircrew of Flight 1549 had excellent communication. Captain Sully attributed this to be one of the main factors to their successful landing. Finally, Captain Wheaton miscalculated the distance and hit a bridge, whereas Captain Sully, an expert pilot, masterfully landed on the river.

The Devil

The devil is involved in a general sense. Death is a result of Adam and Eve's fall, which was caused by the devil tempting them in the Garden of Eden. Romans 6:23 says, "For the wages of sin is death, but the gift of God is eternal life in Christ Jesus our Lord." Paul also writes, "For all have sinned and fallen short of the glory of God" (Romans 3:23). The result of sin is death and the crash resulted in the death of these 78. If the Canada geese had a perspective they would probably view the devil as the U.S. Department of Agriculture, who massacred over 2,000 geese after Flight 1549.

God's Care

God is seen by the rescuers and the brave individuals who risked their own lives to help save those five passengers from the icy Potomac River. These individuals, with their compassion and love, defied evolution and survival of the fittest to demonstrate God's unconditional love.

President Ronald Reagan, in his first State of the Union Address in 1982, talked about Flight 90 and facing crisis: "We find ourselves, if you will, plunged without warning into icy water, where the currents of moral consequence run swift and deep, and where our fellow man and yes, I believe our Maker, are waiting to see whether we will pass the rope!"

In crisis and suffering, do we take hold of the rope and help make God's presence visible with our actions of love? As Paul says, "Praise be to the God and Father of our Lord Jesus Christ, the Father of compassion and the God of all comfort, who comforts us in all our troubles, so that we can comfort those in any trouble with the comfort we ourselves have received from God" (2 Cor. 1:3-4).

God manifests His presence and love in suffering through His people and their love. Paul writes, "But God, who comforts the downcast, comforted us by the coming of Titus" (2 Cor. 7:6). The cure to suffering is to look outward and minister to those around us who are also suffering.

Condition of the Heart

Miracles do not create faith, nor do they prove the existence of God, but they do reveal the condition of our hearts and our beliefs. 2 Chronicles 32:31, "But when envoys were sent by the rulers of Babylon to ask Hezekiah about the miraculous sign that had occurred in the land, God left him to test him and to know everything that was in his heart." It is better to have weak faith in strong ice than strong faith in weak ice.

Presuppositions

Our presuppositions in the tripolarity theory determine if we are able to see the unseen God and His miracles. A presupposition is an elementary assumption, basic commitment, or foundational perspective in terms of which particular experiences and events are interpreted. **GODISNOWHERE** can be read two different ways: **God is now here** or **God is nowhere**. How we read it depends on our presuppositions and beliefs. Oral Roberts said, "Miracles are always coming toward us, but do we have eyes of faith to see them?"

St. Anselm said, "I believe so that I may understand." St. Augustine states, "My faith precedes my reason but it never contradicts or stultifies it." Pascal said, "Faith is God perceived in the heart not by human reason." Dietrich Bonhoeffer wrote, "Only those who believe can obey and only those who obey can believe." These Christian theologians and philosophers agree that belief in God requires a step of faith and also obedience. As we trust in God and obey, He reveals Himself to us and we are able to see His hand in our lives and His creation. Isaiah said, "The Lord has hidden himself from his people but I trust him and place my hope in him" (Isaiah 8:17).

Miracles Require Faith

The miracle on the Hudson and the catastrophe on the Potomac require us to have eyes of faith. We must see God in the midst of His creation operating behind the scenes with grace and redemption. The only verse in the Bible when Jesus is directly addressed as God is in John 20:28 when doubting Thomas placed his hands on Jesus' scars. "Thomas said to Jesus, 'My Lord and my God!' Then Jesus told him, 'Because you have seen me, you have believed; blessed are those who have not seen and yet have believed'" (John 20:28-30). In the midst of tragedy (the death of Jesus), Thomas' faith blossomed (the resurrection).

Ever-present Help

Psalm 46:1-3 says, "God is our refuge and strength, an ever-present help in trouble. Therefore we will not fear, though the earth gives way and the mountains fall into the heart of the sea, though its waters roar and foam and mountains quake with their surging. Selah." God promises He will be an ever-present help in our times of trouble.

Trust

Our response to the hidden God in the tripolarity theory is trust and obedience. Like Job, "Though God slay me, yet will I trust in him; I will surely defend my ways to his face" (Job 13:15). The Prophet Isaiah said, "Who among you fears the Lord and obeys the word of his servant? Let him who walks in the dark, who has no light, trust in the name of the Lord and rely on his God" (Isaiah 50:10).

Summary

Dr. Larry Crabb wrote, "You know you're finding God when you believe that God is good no matter what happens. To believe Christ (faith), to serve Christ and others (love), and to wait for Christ (hope); this is what it means to find God."[19] As we serve hurting people we make God's presence and power visible.

When faced with tragedy we have the choice to seek the invisible God. Eyes of faith and a heart of trust can help us realize that God is now here. Like the father in the Gospel of Mark, we need only to cry out, "Lord, I do believe; help me overcome my unbelief" (Mark 9:24). God was present in the miracle on the Hudson and the catastrophe on the Potomac and faith empowers us to be aware of His presence.

---

[19] Larry Crabb, *Finding God* (Grand Rapids: Zondervan, 1993), 103, 211.

Chapter 3
Love of God

By loving the unlovable, God has made me loveable.

St. Augustine

Love God and do as you please.

St. Augustine

For God so loved the world that he gave his one and only Son, that whoever believes in him shall not perish but have eternal life. For God did not send his Son into the world to condemn the world, but to save the world through him.

John 3:16-17

This is how God showed his love among us: He sent his one and only Son into the world that we might live through him.

1 John 4:9

Introduction

IN SEPTEMBER OF 1980 at Arts and Apples Festival, a woman was selling handmade stuffed prairie dogs; I begged my mom to buy me one of these prairie dogs. On Christmas as I unwrapped my final gift there was Prairie Pup. As eighties kids my brother Chuck and I had Transformers, G.I. Joe, He-Man, and Star Wars figures but the one toy I treasured most was my Prairie Pup. He was only 10 ½ inches tall with soft-as-silk brown fur and a little black mark on his tail. I carried Prairie Pup everywhere; he slept in my bed and he was considered a member of our family.

When I was in fourth grade, my teacher Ms. Milne had the class enter the Detroit Edison Safety Poster Contest. My drawing was of Prairie Pup building a fort near electric lines. This drawing was the winner for my age group and for the prize Prairie Pup and I met NBA Hall of Famer and the Pistons' all-time leader in points and assists, Isiah Thomas.

Prairie and I were inseparable like Linus and his beloved blanket. After sixth grade, as I began playing sports and had an interest in girls, Prairie, now furless from all his years of love, ceased to have his endless travel adventures. Now he sits retired next to my bed. Over the years I have continued to collect prairie dogs and have about one hundred of them. Yet even the newer ones with their realistic fur and bark sounds cannot compare to the love-worn Prairie Pup. What is love? In two words, Prairie Pup.

Meaning of Love

Being loved caused Prairie Pup to lose his soft fur and made him look shabby from years of wear. Zephaniah 3:17 describes God's awesome love for His children: "The Lord your God is with you, he is mighty to save. He will take delight in you, he will quiet you with his love, he will rejoice over you with singing."

Love involves being a part of another person's life and sharing in their experiences and dreams. It requires commitment, faithfulness, empathy, integrity, and transparency. The Apostle Paul in his famous passage on love states, "Love is patient, love is kind. It does not envy, it does not boast, it is not proud. It is not rude, it is not self-seeking, it is not easily angered, it keeps no records of wrongs. Love does not delight in evil but rejoices with the truth. It always protects, always trusts, always hopes, always perseveres. Love never fails" (1 Cor. 13:4-8).

Transforming Love

The world teaches us that to receive love and respect we must be worthy or earn it by our good deeds. As the first-century Roman poet Ovid said, "If you want to be loved, be loveable." This contract style of love is the opposite of God's unconditional love. A Christian marriage counselor once said, "If statements in a relationship are a contract, unconditional love in a relationship is a covenant." "If you cook my meal, I will love you," says the husband to his wife. The wife smiles and says, "Cut the lawn and pay our bills then I will respect you."

Unconditional love says, "I love you for who you are but care too much to leave you that way." Rev. Bob Lee gives us a good definition of love: "Love is an unconditional commitment to an imperfect person."[20]

The Apostle Paul describes God's unconditional love for us: "You see, at just the right time, when we were still powerless, Christ died for the ungodly. Very rarely will anyone die for a righteous man, though for a good man someone might possibly dare to die. But God demonstrates his own love for us in this: While we were still sinners, Christ died for us" (Rom. 5:6-8).

Woman at the Well

Jewish historian Josephus wrote in *Antiquities of the Jews*, "Every pious Jew traveling to Galilee had to go around Samaria." The most direct and quickest route to Galilee is through Samaria. The Jews' hostility toward the Samaritans caused them to travel extra miles to avoid the Samaritans' unclean presence. They perceived the Samaritans as unclean for four main reasons. **First**, they intermarried among the Gentiles and were termed by the Jews as half-breeds and dogs. **Second**, in 931 B.C., when the kingdom of Israel divided, they followed the leadership of Jeroboam, King David's former military advisor (northern kingdom), instead of King Rehoboam, the son of

---

[20] Philip Yancey, *After the Wedding* (Waco: Word Books, 1976), 32.

King Solomon (southern kingdom). Under Jeroboam's rule they constructed and worshipped a golden calf in the city of Dan. **Third**, in the second century B.C. under Antiochus Epiphanes of the Seleucid Empire, the Samaritans helped his Hellenization process by attending the coliseum events and assimilating by intermarriage. The Jews referred to Epiphanes as Epimanes (the Mad One), they revolted under the leadership of the Maccabees and overthrew his oppressive domain.

The **final** offense and greatest was that the Samaritans worshipped on Mount Gerizim instead of Jerusalem. The Samaritan woman said to Jesus, "Our fathers worshipped on this mountain, but you Jews claim that the place where we must worship is in Jerusalem" (John 4:20). Jesus responded, "Yet a time is coming and has now come when the true worshippers will worship the Father in spirit and truth, for they are the kind of worshippers the Father seeks" (John 4:23).

John wrote in his narrative on the Samaritan woman at the well, "Now Jesus had to go through Samaria" (John 4:4). Unlike the Jews of His day, Jesus, compelled by the Father's love, went through Samaria. 2 Chronicles 16:9 says, "The eyes of the Lord range throughout the earth to strengthen those whose hearts are fully committed to him." A great revival had already occurred in Galilee and many Jews had repented and were baptized (John 4:1-3). Jesus was not expedient to attend this revival among His people but took precious time to visit a spiritually hungry and outcast Samaritan woman. Jesus approached her with respect and even asked her for a drink of water. This behavior broke every Jewish cultural norm and demonstrated that God does not examine the outward appearance but the heart.

This woman had been married five times and her current man (number six), with whom she lived was not her husband. In Jewish numerology the number six symbolizes "unrest or unease—sinfulness." St. Augustine said, "The heart remains restless until it finds rest in God." The Samaritan woman was in an adulterous relationship with her boyfriend (man number six). The number seven symbolizes perfection and the seventh man whom she met was Jesus, the only perfect one. The gospel of John heightens this motif (seven) by connecting the woman at the well narrative with the healing of the royal official's son.

John 5:51-53 states, "While he was still on the way, his servants met him with the news that his boy was living. When he inquired as to the time when his son got better, they said to him, "The fever left him yesterday at the seventh hour." Then the father realized that this was the exact time at which Jesus said to him, "Your son will live." So he and all his household believed." These two passages combined with the miracle of the water turned into wine reiterate the motifs— belief and faith (John 2:11, 4:42, 4:53). For John's audience in Ephesus, to see Jesus is to believe (John 20:28-31).

Jesus saw this woman's thirst for love and offered her the water of life. Søren Kierkegaard said, "Longing is the umbilical cord of the higher life." Jesus did not condemn her for the five failed marriages and her adulterous relationship. Instead, He offered the hope of redemption to fill her heart's longing for unconditional love.

The Samaritan woman was rejected by her people and this caused her to draw water during the heat of the day. Jesus also experienced rejection from His own people and understood her pain (John 1:11). She was searching for love through relationships with men rather than the true source, God. I love the words she used in her evangelistic message, "Come, see a man!" (John 4:29). We can picture the other Samaritan women looking at her, shaking their heads, and with laughter in their voice saying, "Yeah, you have said these same words six times before and all those men have been losers!"

Jesus' love transformed her from an outcast into a powerful evangelist. John 4:28 states, "Then, leaving her water jar, the woman went back to the town and said to the people . . ." As the disciples Peter and John left their nets to follow Jesus so this woman left her water jar. She no longer had fear but with boldness testified Jesus was the Messiah. John concludes his narrative stating, "Many of the Samaritans from that town believed because of the woman's testimony, 'He told me everything I ever did'" (John 4:29).

Whole-hearted Commitment

Unlike the Samaritan woman at the well who gave her whole life to Jesus, the Jews in Galilee attempted to make Jesus their conquering king (John 6:15). This multitude in Galilee refused to accept Jesus whole-heartedly and turned from Him because His teaching demanded their total allegiance. Jesus withdrew from their presence but He drew near to the woman at the well. Jesus told her, "The Father seeks those who will worship Him in spirit and truth." Jesus sought her out because she was willing to leave everything for Him.

Complete Devotion

The love of God in the tripolarity theory demands we give Christ our whole heart and devotion. The Samaritan woman had a life-changing encounter with Jesus because her heart was open to Christ's love. The great multitude in Galilee, like the rich young ruler, missed experiencing God because they refused to forsake all for the kingdom of God.

The rich young ruler in Mark's gospel had all the outward signs of a true seeker of God (Mark 10:17-31). In Jewish Deuteronomistic theology wealth was a sign of God's blessing and covenant (Deut. 11 and 28). He approached Jesus with reverence and bowed before Him and acknowledged Christ's teachings to have divine authority. He was confident and truly believed he was in a right relationship with God as he said, "All these commandments I have kept!" Mark records Jesus' response, "Jesus looked at him and loved him. 'One thing you lack,' he said. 'Go, sell everything you have and give to the poor, and you will have treasure in heaven. Then come, follow me'" (Mark 10:21). Jesus' demand he forsake everything and follow Him revealed his true love and devotion.

This young man's great wealth had become in his heart an idol and his god. The Prophet Jeremiah warned, "Do men make their own gods? Yes, but they are not gods!" (Jerm. 16:20). John Bevere said, "An idol is anything we love, trust in, or give our attention to before God." Larry W. Hurtado wrote, "This rich man's interest in the next world was not sincere enough to enable him to give up his preoccupation with this world."

Perverted Love

The rich man's love had become perverted as he trusted in his earthly treasures instead of God. As Deuteronomy 8:17-18 states, "You may say to yourself, 'My power and the strength of my hands have produced this wealth for me' (internal locus). But remember the Lord your God, for it is he who gives us the ability to produce wealth, and so confirms his covenant (external locus)." St. Augustine in *The City of God* describes this perverted love leading to idolatry with the example of lust and greed. One person examines a beautiful woman with love and wants to marry her and have a family, another lusts after her and only desires kinky sex and self-pleasure. It is not the woman's beauty that is perverse but the beholder. Another person has greed for the riches of gold and covets it, while someone else desires the gold to feed their family of five from the gold's intrinsic value. St. Augustine writes, "Thus, greed is not a defect in the gold desired but in the one who loves it perversely nor is lust a defect in bodies which are beautiful and pleasing; it's a sin in the soul of the one who loves corporal pleasures perversely." This corrupted love deceived the rich young ruler and made him believe he was serving God while his real master was himself.

Two Masters

The Apostle Paul said, "Do I mean then that a sacrifice offered to an idol is anything, or that an idol is anything? No, but the sacrifices of pagans are offered to demons, not to God, and I do not want you to be participants with demons. You cannot drink the cup of the Lord and the cup of demons too; you cannot have a part in both the Lord's table and the table of demons" (1 Cor. 10:19-21). The worship of idols, "anything we love or place before God," according to Paul, is the same as giving our heart's devotion and allegiance to the devil and his horde of demons, since he is the god of this age.

Jeffrey Burton Russell wrote concerning the apostolic fathers' view of pagan idol worship, "Sacrifice to an idol was not a silly foible, but an act of worship of the devil, a blasphemy against Christ, a deed worthy of damnation. The serpent is involved in the idolatrous rites of pagans."[21]

Jesus in the Sermon on the Mount warned, "No one can serve two masters. Either he will hate the one and love the other, or he will be devoted to the one and despise the other. You cannot serve both God and money" (Matt. 6:24). The devil in the tripolarity theory attempts to bring bondage into our lives by leading us astray by other masters. These other masters or idols can include false beliefs and addictions to sex, drugs, alcohol, money, or even good things like our jobs or friends. Anything we put above serving God and instant obedience to Him is our true master and lord.

If we serve these masters instead of the true Master then we will be enslaved by them and hindered from experiencing God's love and grace which sets us free. Paul warned the Corinthians of this condition, "You know that when you were pagans, somehow or other you were influenced and led astray to mute idols" (1 Cor. 12:2). 2 Corinthians 11:3 also reiterates, "But I am afraid that just as Eve was deceived by the serpent's cunning, your minds may somehow be led astray from your sincere and pure devotion to Christ."

Hardened Heart

When we allow our hearts to become hardened we become dead to the things of God. The Apostle Paul wrote, "They are darkened in their understanding and separated from the life of God because of

---

[21] Jeffrey Burton Russell, *Satan: The Early Christian Tradition* (Ithaca and London: Cornell University Press, 1981), 70.

the ignorance that is in them due to the hardening of their hearts" (Eph. 4:18). Those who choose to allow their hearts to become hardened by disobedience become like Jim's heatless dryer.

Jim noticed that the dryer in his basement was not operating properly as his jeans were still soaking wet after 40 minutes on high heat. He checked every electric wire on the machine and discovered they were functioning properly so he decided to check the duct that brings the heat into the dryer. While checking it, he discovered a robin's nest which blocked the flow. This bird's nest did not form *ex nihilo*, "out of nothing," but one branch and twig at a time. In the same way, a hard heart also forms over time; a bad attitude at work and a branch of rebellion is added, or heartbreak from a relationship gone sour and a couple more branches of bitterness form, or lustful desires left uncontrolled and we add more mud and twigs to the mix, until our hearts have become hardened. As the robin's nest blocked the flow of heat so the dryer was unable to operate, so a hardened heart hinders the flow of God's power in our lives.

Bitterness and selfish ambitions are the fruits of the devil that enslave and lead us away from our pure love for Christ. As James said, "But if you harbor bitter envy and selfish ambition in your hearts, do not boast about it or deny the truth. Such "wisdom" does not come down from heaven but is earthly, unspiritual, of the devil" (James 3:14-15).

Led Astray

The devil leads humanity astray by directing their hearts' affections away from God. As believers draw near to God their desires become like His. But if we choose to love the world instead, we become open to the devil's deception which leads to death. In South America poachers trap and kill howler monkeys by cutting a hole in a coconut and placing a coin in the center. The hole is just big enough for the howler monkey to put their hand in and take it out. Due to the tiny size of the holes, if the howler monkey grasps the coin, they will be unable to remove their hand, unless they release the coin.

The poachers wait in the bush for the monkey to grab the coined coconut, then they proceed to club them to death. These monkeys could easily escape the murderous poachers if they only would choose to let loose the precious coins. The monkeys' love for this worthless treasure causes them to refuse to let go. The devil, like these poachers, uses our misdirected desires to lead us astray from God's perfect love.

Love God & Be Free

The love of God sets us free to obey His commands and fulfill His purpose. Jesus said, "For where your treasure is, there your heart will be also" (Matt. 6:21). If we love God then we will have a heart's desire to please and obey Him (John 14:23). A man who truly loves and cares about his wife and children will have a desire to do what is in their best interests and not harm them by his actions. This man can love his family and do as he pleases because it pleases him to serve them. The greatest commandment is to love God with our whole heart and the second is to love our neighbor as ourselves (Matt. 22:37-40). This love sets us free from selfish ambition, materialism, and greed, to serve God with sincere hearts.

The definitive test that we love God is obedience and love for others. 1 John 3:10 says, "This is how we know who the children of God are and who the children of the devil are: Anyone who does not do what is right is not a child of God; nor is anyone who does not love his brother."

Summary

What is love? A heart's desire to serve and obey God and love others. In the tripolarity theory, we have a choice to either serve ourselves or God. God's love requires us to lay down our lives and take up the cross and follow Him. As we follow God and obey Him, He creates in us love.

Chapter 4
Origin of the Devil

Expecting the devil to fight fair because you are a good Christian is like expecting the bull not to charge because you are a vegetarian.

Anonymous

Your hideous face composed of lust and filth and gibberish sweeps all doubts away—all. Since the devil exists, God also exists. Otherwise you would have won a long time ago.

> Father Riccardo, as he confronts the German exterminator of the Jews in Rolf Hochhuth's *The Deputy.*

Be self-controlled and alert. Your enemy the devil prowls around like a roaring lion looking for someone to devour. Resist him, standing firm in the faith, because you know that your brothers throughout the world are undergoing the same kind of sufferings.

1 Peter 5:8-9

But even the archangel Michael, when he was disputing with the devil about the body of Moses, did not dare bring a slanderous accusation against him, but said, "The Lord rebuke you!"

Jude 9

Introduction

ASTRONAUT SCOTT KELLY (the brother-in-law of Congresswoman Gabrielle Giffords) in response to the lurid Arizona shooting on January 8, 2011, that killed six including a nine-year-old girl and severely injured his brother's wife, reported from the International Space Station:

"We have a unique vantage point from the International Space Station. As I look out the window, I see a very beautiful planet earth that seems very inviting and peaceful. Unfortunately, it is not. These days we are constantly reminded of the unspeakable acts of violence, horror and damage we can inflict upon one another, not just with our actions, but also with our irresponsible words. We are better than this, we must do better."[22]

God created the earth to be a peaceful and inhabitable planet. The Creator describes His masterpiece of creation humanity, "Very good!" Adam and Eve were created in the image of God; they were innocent of sin before they chose to eat the fruit of the tree of knowledge of good and evil.

The devil and disobedience to God have infested with evil this once peaceful planet. The world then fell from its innocence into violence. The Bible, like a flight data recorder on an airplane, gives an explanation of the catastrophe on this planet. 1 John 3:8 says, "He who does what is sinful is of the devil, because the devil has been sinning from the beginning. The reason the Son of God appeared was to destroy the devil's work."

The Devil's Origin

St. Augustine said, "Do you seek to know the origin of the devil? It is the same as that of the other angels. But the other angels persevered in their obedience, whereas he, by disobeying, and being proud, fell and became the devil."

---

[22] http://www1.whdh.com/news/articles/national/12003239626798/gifford-s-brother-in-law-s... 1/14/2011

According to Jewish tradition, Midrash interpretation, and rabbis' teachings, the serpent Satan was the accuser and tempter of humanity and the key prosecutor before God's judgment seat. The Hebrew word for Satan means "accuser or slanderer," as demonstrated in Zechariah 3:1: "Then he showed me Joshua the high priest standing before the angel of the Lord, and Satan standing at his right side to accuse him." Rabbis have interpreted Satan as the accuser of the brothers, and the tempter of the faithful based on his accusations against Job (Job 1:9-11).

The devil according to church history was a guardian cherub; a type of angel who, by the pride of his beauty and splendor, tried to ascend into heaven and rebel against God. A cherub or seraph, according to ancient Egyptian's history and hieroglyphs, was a winged cobra. The rearing winged cobras, the Uraeus and Wadjet, in ancient hieroglyphs were depicted as facing Ra, the sun-god, with their wings opened wide, stealing the glory of his sun rays. Uraeus was positioned with wings opened wide above Ra on the headdress of pharaohs and ornaments, symbolizing an ascent for divine authority. It is interesting to note that in Isaiah 6:2, the seraphs covered their faces in the presence of God and gave Him glory, saying, "Holy, holy, holy is the Lord Almighty; the whole earth is full of his glory." This was the exact opposite response of the winged cobras, Uraeus & Wadjet; their wings were wide open, and basking in the divine glory.

The Uraeus symbolized sovereignty and divine authority. These were the very divine attributes which the devil attempted to receive by ascending into heaven and he promised to Jesus if he would bow down and worship him (Matt. 4). The divine power and authority were also the very qualities the demons recognized and coveted in Jesus' public ministry (Mark 1:24; 5:7). Isaiah 14:29 connects the seraph with the imagery of the Uraeus: "Rejoice not, all you of Philistia, because the rod that struck you is broken; for out of the serpent's root shall come forth a pit viper, and his offspring shall be a flying serpent."

While on the other side of the world in 900 B.C., the Aztec civilizations in Mesoamerica made sacrifices to the Quetzalcoatl, the serpent deity. In the Nahuatl language, *Quetzalcoatl* means "feathered serpent" and was the deity of merchants, crafts, wind, Venus, and knowledge. This feathered serpent was one of the four sons of the deities, Ometecuhti and Omecihuatl, and was referred to as the god of the morning star.

The title, morning star, is the same name that the Prophet Isaiah used for the devil when he attempted to ascend to the throne of God in rebellion.[23] Isaiah 14:12 says, "How you have fallen from heaven O morning star, son of the dawn! You have been cast down to the earth, you who once laid low the nations." When Christ defeated sin and death at the cross, and conquered Satan with his principalities, he took the title morning star and bestowed it on the persecuted believers who overcame the devil. Revelation 2:26 says to those overcomers in the Church of Thyatira, "I will also give him the morning star."

Rebellion

Satan was a worship leader in heaven before his rebellion that caused a third of the angels to turn from God and become evil spirits called demons. Isaiah 14:11 states, "All your pomp has been brought down to the gravel, along with the noise of your harps." The nine jewels the Prophet Ezekiel states adorned the devil in the Garden of Eden were nine of the twelve precious gems on the vestment of the high priest (Ezekiel 28:13; Exodus 28:15-30). In the LXX Septuagint version of Ezekiel 28:13, all twelve precious stones are included. This demonstrates that the devil held a priestly worship office in heaven before his fall. In Judaism, Christianity, and Islam the serpent was considered an evil villain and traitor. In almost all the other ancient religions and cultures serpents were worshipped and revered as divine.

---

[23] See endnotes: Morning Star.

Revelation 12:4 says, "His (devil) tail swept a third of the stars out of the sky and flung them to the earth. The dragon stood in front of the woman who was about to give birth, so that he might devour her child the moment it was born." A third of the angels rebelled with Satan and they compose his army of demonic forces. These fallen angels are involved in the cosmic battle between the Kingdom of Light and the Kingdom of Darkness.

As the period of Satan's reign of terror nears its consummation with Christ's return, the devil implements greater deception on the laboring earth. Isaiah prophesied, "See, darkness covers the earth and thick darkness is over the peoples, but the Lord rises upon you and his glory appears over you" (Isaiah 60:2).

Rabbi Abraham Heschel said, "The Talmud teaches that the greater or more powerful the man, the greater his evil inclination or his ability for good." The Apostle John said, "Woe to the earth and the sea, because the devil has gone down to you! He is filled with fury, because he knows that his time is short" (Rev. 12:12).

The good news for the believer is as the day of the Lord draws near, God pours His Spirit in a greater measure upon the earth and gives us more grace to stand. Our lights shine at their brightest in the pitch black. Romans 5:20 states, "The law was added so that the trespass might increase. But where sin increased, grace increased all the more." Jesus said, "For the one whom God has sent speaks the words of God, for God gives the Spirit without limit" (John 3:34). The Prophet Joel said in the last days the Lord will pour out his Spirit on all people and the sun and moon will be transformed into darkness (Joel 2:28-32).

This outpouring of the Holy Spirit in the last days will result in a great harvest of souls from every people, tribe, tongue, and nation as the Apostle John described in Revelation 7:9-17. John 16:8 says, "When the Holy Spirit comes, he will convict the world of guilt in regard to sin and righteousness and judgment." The Holy Spirit guides people to Christ and removes the blinders of the devil from the unbelievers.

Devil's Fall

St. Augustine said,

> "Deceived by himself, the devil longs to deceive another. He has become an enemy of our human race, the inventor of death, the teacher of pride, the origin of malice, the chief of criminals, the prince of all vice, the promoter of base passions. Because of this, when he beheld the first man God made, Adam, the father of us all, and saw man made from the muck of the earth in the image of God, and adorned with modesty, gifted with temperance, surrounded with love, robed in immortality, he grew jealous and envious that man had received the great blessing which he himself had as an angel, as he realized, and lost through pride. Instantly he became envious and, insatiable killer of men that he was, he stole the blessings from our first parents and brought us all to destruction."

Tertullian in the second century connects Isaiah 14 and Ezekiel 28 with the devil's rebellion and writes,

> "What was the origin of this malice of lying and deceit toward men, and slandering of God? Most certainly not from God, who made the angel good like all his works. Indeed, before he became the devil, he is declared to be the wisest of all; and wisdom is surely no evil. If you turn to the prophecy of Ezekiel, you will easily perceive that this angel was both by creation good and by his own act corrupt."

Jesus' mission on earth was to restore creation from the effects of the fall through His death and resurrection and to bring humanity into reconciliation with the Father. Hebrews 2:14-15 says, "Since the children have flesh and blood, he too shared in their humanity so that by his death he might destroy him who holds the power of death—that is, the devil—and free those who all their lives were held in slavery by their fear of death."

In Genesis chapter 3, the devil makes his first appearance in the Garden of Eden, as a serpent, and tempts Eve to eat the fruit from the tree of knowledge of good and evil. The devil deceived Eve by stating, "For God knows that when you eat of it your eyes will be opened, and you will be like God, knowing good and evil." Satan promised Eve the tree would give her freedom and make her all powerful like God.

Francis A. Schaeffer said, "Every human problem stems from humanity striving to make something autonomous from God and as soon as anything is made autonomous from God, then nature eats up grace."[24] The devil's prideful attempt to ascend into heaven for God's throne led to his fall from heaven to the natural world (Isaiah 14:9-16, Ezekiel 28:1-19).

Adam and Eve's disobedience of God's command was the cause of the fall. Nature ate up grace by their choice to eat the fruit. God warned Adam, "For when you eat of it you will surely die!" (Gen. 2:17). Eve was deceived by the serpent's cunning and ate (1Tim. 2:14). Adam, by his own free will combined with his wife's persuasion, also ate.

Genesis 3:6 describes Eve's response to the devil's diabolic proposal, "When Eve saw that the fruit of the tree was good for food and pleasing to the eye, and also desirable for gaining wisdom, she took some and ate it. She also gave some to her husband, who was with her, and he also ate."

Death was not instant like Zeus' lightning bolt but they were separated from the presence of God. Their eating of the fruit banished them from the Garden of Eden and death arrived shortly after when their son Cain brutally murdered his brother Abel over religious sacrifices. Sin never stays small.

---

[24] Francis A. Schaeffer, *He Is There and He Is Not Silent* (Wheaton: Tyndale House, 1972), 82.

Grace

God responded to humanity's disobedience with grace and He covered their sins with a blood sacrifice. Genesis 3:21 states, "The Lord God made garments of skin for Adam and his wife and clothed them." Adam and Eve, in fear and shame, attempted to hide from the presence of God because of their nakedness. They clothed themselves with fig leaves (nature), but the Father covered their sins with grace.

God promised them a future victory over the serpent in Genesis 3:15: "And I will put enmity between you (the devil) and the woman, and between your offspring (seed) and hers; he (Christ) will crush your head, and you will strike his heel." Christ's bruised heel from the devil led to His resurrection and ascension. Satan's crushed head from Christ resulted in him being terminally ill and his ultimate future punishment will be banishment forever into the Lake of Fire.

Christ's Blood

Jesus' death on the cross brought salvation to the believer. Zechariah 9:11 says, "As for you, because of the blood of my covenant with you, I will free your prisoners from the waterless pit." Acts 20:28 says, "Be shepherds of the church of God, which he bought with his own blood." Only blood is able to cover our sins and empower us to live free of its enslavement. Leviticus 17:11 states, "For the life of the creature is in the blood, and I have given it to you to make atonement for yourselves on the altar; it is the blood that makes atonement for one's life."

Jesus' death was the perfect sacrifice and defeated the devil. Hebrews 12:24 says, "To Jesus the mediator of a new covenant, and to the sprinkled blood that speaks a better word than the blood of Abel." It speaks a better word since the blood of Christ gives us victory over death and sets us free from sin and the power of the devil. Revelation 12:11 says, "They overcame the devil by the blood of the Lamb and the word of their testimony; they did not love their lives so as to shrink from death."

Deception

The devil deceives us just as he did with our great-grandparents, Adam and Eve; Satan makes sin appear enjoyable as he attempts to lead us astray from God's grace. The Apostle Paul warns, "And no wonder, for Satan himself masquerades as an angel of light" (2 Cor. 11:14).

St Augustine in *Faith, Hope, and Charity* (16:60) stated, "The greater is the need to discern and recognize Satan when he transforms himself, as it were, into an angel of light, lest he should deceive and seduce us into doing something sinful . . . But how many people are there who are prepared to escape all his death dealing whiles, unless God watches over them and keeps them from going astray?"

Isaiah 5:20 describes the devil's mission statement: "Who to those who call evil good and good evil, who put darkness for light and light for darkness, who put bitter for sweet and sweet for bitter."

There's an old preacher joke about an agnostic who died and met St. Peter at the pearly gates and received a free afterlife tour. Peter said to the agnostic, "Do you want to enter heaven or hell for eternity? The agnostic said, "Since I am an agnostic I don't know what I believe so do you think that you could give me a tour of both so I make the wise decision?" "Sure!" Peter replied. The agnostic then entered a glass elevator and Peter pressed a button. The elevator proceeded downward for 20 minutes.

The door opened, and to the agnostic's amazement he saw millions of beautiful babes in bikinis drinking cold beer on a beach. The agnostic reentered the glass elevator a couple minutes later with a beer in hand and the elevator began to move toward heaven and the agnostic looked up and the sky appeared blurry. The agnostic said to St. Peter, "I don't really need the heavenly tour; hell seems great with all the free beer and endless selection of women! It was not a lake of fire, like I was taught in Sunday school, the few times that I went. So beam me down, Scotty!" A few seconds later, the agnostic was screaming and gnashing his teeth, in a lake of fire, yelling, "Where's the beer and the women?" Peter replied, "You saw Hell's advertising department!"

The love of the world causes our hearts to become calloused toward God and to be selfish toward others. Sin distorts the voice of God, His character, and our relationship with Him. James, the Lord's brother, said, "You adulterous people, don't you know that friendship with the world is hatred toward God? Anyone who chooses (internal locus) to become a friend of the world becomes an enemy of God" (James 4:4).

Devil's Lie

The devil's greatest lie is that he and God do not exist and the highest aim in life is fulfilling our own pleasures. Like the Greek philosopher Protagoras (490-420 B.C.) said, "Man is the measure of all things." The insidious operation of the devil in the tripolarity theory is to deceive humanity into believing he does not exist and that God is a fictional character created out of our imagination.

Spiritual Warfare

Shortly after the tragedy of September 11, Johnny Knoxville from the MTV program *Jackass* put on a red devil's outfit and walked around New York City with a pitchfork and jumbo sign that read, "I am not responsible for September 11 because I was on vacation in Hawaii!" An angry mob of New Yorkers quickly descended on the scene and began to beat Johnny the Jackal. Johnny, at the end of this disturbing video, was running for his dear life.

The devil's greatest weapon is to cause people not to believe in his existence. If we, like those angry New Yorkers, saw a visible devil, we would be vigilant and fight him tooth and nail. John Bevere writes, "We must remember that the devil doesn't come with a pitchfork, a pointed tail, and horns, saying, 'I'm the devil, and I've come to steal the Word of God and destroy your life!' If he did, most would firmly resist and believe even more in the supernatural realm."[25]

Luke 12:39 states, "Understand this: if the owner of the house had known what hour the thief was coming, he would not have let his house be broken into." A belief in the devil causes us to understand we are in a cosmic war with unseen spiritual forces and we must not allow these evil influences to have access to our lives. Ephesians 4:27 says, "And do not give the devil a foothold."

The Apostle Paul said, "For though we live in the world, we do not wage war as the world does. The weapons we fight with are not the weapons of the world. On the contrary, they have divine power to demolish strongholds. We demolish arguments and every pretense that sets itself up against the knowledge of God, and take captive every thought to make it obedient to Christ" (2 Cor. 10:3-5).

Resist the Devil

The believer's response to the spiritual forces of evil is to trust God and resist the devil by prayer and obedience. The Apostle James wrote, "Submit yourselves, then, to God. Resist the devil, and he will flee from you. Come near to God and he will come near to you. Wash your hands, you sinners, and purify your hearts, you double-minded" (James 4:7-8).

Our relationship with God gives us authority over Satan and his demonic forces. In James 4:7 the word for flee, θευξεται, is associated with a fugitive running from the law. As we resist the devil, he must flee from us like a criminal who takes flight when he sees the sheriff armed with a gun. As John of the Cross said, "The devil fears a soul united to God as he does God himself."

The key for victory over the unseen evil forces is to oppose the devil. As believers, we have a choice to gratify the desires of the flesh or live by the Holy Spirit and overcome sin by Christ's empowering

---

[25] John Bevere, *Extraordinary* (Colorado Springs: WaterBrook Press, 2009), 178.

grace. King David said, "Let those who love the Lord hate evil, for he guards the lives of his faithful ones and delivers them from the hand of the wicked" (Psalm 97:10).

Summary

God has given us the victory over spiritual forces. Isaiah 54:17 says, "No weapon forged against you will prevail, and you will refute every tongue that accuses (Satan) you. This is the heritage of the servants of the Lord; this is their vindication from me." Isaiah also said, "When the enemy comes in like a flood, the Spirit of God will raise up a standard against him" (Isaiah 59:19).

In the next two chapters we will examine the devil's insidious operations as he attacks like a flashflood leaving an aftermath of destruction. What makes the devil so satanic is that he is the apostle of futility—everything he does is ultimately destined to fail.

Chapter 5
Insidious Operation of the Devil:
Part 1 (Judas Iscariot)

For if Christ does not grant us power and grace, then the Judas in us betrays Him.

If we depart a little away from Him, the Peter in us sleeps.

St. Jerome

The demonic manifests itself most clearly only when it is in contact with the good.

Søren Kierkegaard

As soon as Judas had taken the bread, he went out. And it was night.

John 13:30

The light shines in the darkness, but the darkness has not understood it.

John 1:5

Introduction

IN THE PREVIOUS CHAPTER, we saw that the devil is the origin of sin, while humanity is held responsible as a secondary causation by our willful choice to disobey God. Insidious is the perfect adjective to convey the devil's mission. The etymology of "insidious" is from the Latin word *insidiosus* and is derived from the two Latin terms *insidia*, meaning "to ambush," combined with *insidere*, meaning "to lie in wait for prey." In modern English insidious can mean "stealthily, treacherous, and crafty."

These are the same adjectives that the Apostle Paul used to describe Elymas the sorcerer who was deceitful like the devil and tried to lead believers away from the faith by his cunning magic. Paul said, "You are a child of the devil and enemy of everything that is right! You are full of all kinds of deceit and trickery. Will you never stop perverting the right ways of the Lord?" (Acts 13:10).

The term "insidious disease" means "an illness that develops so gradually as to be well established before it becomes apparent." For example, the majority of people with an insidious disease have no knowledge they are infected until it is too late. The devil operates by the same manner. Slowly he tries to lead us away from God's grace a little step of disobedience at a time, or he enslaves us through one wrong decision of giving in to temptation leading to another until we are held in chains.

Judas' Betrayal

In the tripolarity theory, Satan's insidious operations were demonstrated by Judas' betrayal of Jesus at the opportune time. Galatians 4:4 says, "But when the time had fully come, God sent his Son." The Father chose at the fullness of time (καιρος) to send Jesus. There are three main Koine Greek words for time: καιρος, χρονοζ, ωρα. In the text above the Apostle Paul used καιρος, "meaning season, divine time, opportune." Χρονοζ refers to chronological or sequential time and is derived from the Greek incorporeal god Chronos, better known as Father Time. The third term ωρα simply means "hour, moment, or occasion."

The insidious operation of the devil is he is patiently waiting for the opportune time to wreak his diabolic destruction, like a lion in the bush, stalking its prey. After Jesus passed the temptations in the desert, revealing His identity as the Son of God, Luke concluded his temptation narrative stating, "When the devil had finished all this tempting, he left Jesus until an opportune time (καιρος)" (Luke 4:11).

The opportune time arrived unexpectedly three and a half years later as Judas prepared to betray Jesus in the Upper Room at the Last Supper. Luke writes,

> "Then Satan entered Judas called Iscariot, one of the Twelve. And Judas went to the chief priests and the officers of the temple guard and discussed with them how he might betray Jesus. They were delighted and agreed to give him money. He consented, and watched for an opportunity to hand Jesus over to them when no crowd was present" (Luke 22:3-6).

Satan entered Judas at the opportune time (ευκαιρος) as Judas had willfully chosen to betray Christ to the religious leaders. ευκαιρος is also translated as "opportune time" in Mark 6:21; King Herod's birthday was the perfect occasion for Herodias' operation to take her revenge on John the Baptist by having him beheaded for calling her husband an adulterer (Mark 6:19-27). John the Baptist's death, as the one who prepares the way for the Messiah, foreshadowed Jesus' crucifixion. The gospel writers demonstrate this correlation by using the Greek word παρεδιδου, meaning to hand over or to deliver in both death narrative accounts (Mark 1:14; 15:15, Luke 22:6).

The earliest historical source of the betrayal of Jesus in the New Testament is 1 Corinthians 11:23-24: "For I received from the Lord that which I also handed over to you, that the Lord Jesus, on the night in which he was betrayed (παραδιδομι), took bread, and after giving thanks broke it and said, 'This is my body given for you.'" We can interpret παραδιδομι in this text as both "betrayed"—Judas Iscariot was the nefarious agent who betrayed Christ; and "handed over"—God was the agent that handed Christ over to be crucified for our sins.

Judas' Choice

Judas' decision to betray Jesus demonstrates human free will in the tripolarity theory.[26] The Jewish historian Josephus wrote, "A Zealot will never call anyone lord or master." Judas was a Zealot and, in the gospels, every time he addressed Jesus he referred to Him as teacher or rabbi but never as Lord and Savior.[27] Pastor John MacArthur wrote, "The signature of saving faith is the surrender to the Lordship of Jesus Christ. The definitive test of true discipleship is a willingness to bow to His authority."[28]

Judas, a first-century Jewish name, conveyed the symbolism of the national hero and revolutionary Judas the Hammer (Judah) from the Maccabean Revolt (166-160 B.C.). This revolt resulted in overthrow of the Seleucid Empire in Judah. The term "Maccabees" was used to describe the Jewish guerrilla warfare tactics and is derived from the Hebrew word for hammer. Judas is acclaimed as one of the greatest warriors in Jewish history alongside Joshua, Gideon, and King David. The Jewish feast Hanukkah (Dedication) commemorates the re-dedication of temple worship in Jerusalem in 165 B.C., after Judas with his brothers removed the pagan Zeus statuary.

1 Maccabees 3:25-26 describes Judas' great exploits, "Then Judas and his brothers began to be feared, and terror fell on the Gentiles all around them. His fame reached the king and the Gentiles talked of the battles of Judas." At Judas Maccabeus' death the Jews lamented and said, "How is the mighty fallen, the savior of Israel." The writer of 1 Maccabees concludes his record on Judas stating, "Now the rest of the acts of Judas, and his wars and the brave deeds that he did,

---

[26] See endnotes: Judas Iscariot's motive in the Gospel of Matthew for betraying Christ.

[27] Luke Timothy Johnson, *Living Jesus* (San Francisco: Harper Collins, 1999), 150.

[28] John MacArthur, *The Gospel According to Jesus* (Grand Rapids: Zondervan, 1988), 203-210.

and his greatness, have not been recorded, but they were many" (1 Maccabees 9:22).

In Judas Iscariot's household, his parents would have retold the epic battles of the Maccabees with pride, and his heart would have longed for a contemporized revolt against the Roman Empire with him as a commanding officer in this revolt to freedom. The motif of Judas would have the pejorative of traitor and terrorist to the Gentiles in the city of Rome to whom Mark wrote his gospel.

The Zealots

The Zealots movement was founded in A.D. 6 by Judas the Galilean and the Pharisee Saddok. The census order by Caesar Augustus in A.D. 6 and Judaea and Samaria placed under direct Roman rule were the immediate cause of the founding of this nationalistic religious movement. According to Josephus, Judas the Galilean exhorted his countrymen not to pay Roman tribute since Yahweh was Israel's only absolute sovereign king and lord, not Caesar. Josephus regarded Judas the Galilean followers as brigands (λῃσταὶ) the same opprobrious term used in the Gospel of John for the insurrectionist Barabbas.

Mark 11:17 uses this same term to express thieves in the Temple at Jerusalem: "Is it not written, 'My house will be called a house of prayer for all nations? But you have made it a den of (λῃστῶν) robbers.'" During the siege, the Temple had been the chief citadel of Jewish resistance and it had been held by Zealots, who in Roman eyes and Mark's Sitz im Leben were λῃσταὶ (brigands and robbers).

The Zealots viewed themselves as a prototype of Phinehas, the grandson of Aaron and the son of the High Priest Eleazar, a leader commissioned by Moses to lead Israel in a holy war of revenge against the Midianites and their idolatrous practices (Numbers 25:1-18). Judas the Galilean and his Zealots would never touch a coin with an engraved image.[29] The Jewish desire for freedom found

---

[29] S.G.F. Brandon, *Jesus and the Zealots* (Manchester: Manchester University Press, 1967), 45.

expression on the coins issued during the Jewish revolt of A.D. 66-70; the inscriptions of some coins read: "for the Redemption of Zion" and "Freedom of Zion."[30]

One of the episodes preceding Judas Iscariot's betrayal in the Synoptic Gospels was Jesus' confrontation with the Pharisees over paying taxes to Rome (Matthew 22:15-22, Mark 12:13-17, Luke 20:20-26). Jesus concluded this heated debate stating, "Give to Caesar what is Caesar's and to God what is God's" (Mark 14:17). This answer would have infuriated a first-century Zealot and made them reject His teachings. In the Acts of the Apostles, Gamaliel the Elder records Judas Galilean's fate: "After him [i.e. Theudas], Judas the Galilean appeared in the days of the census and led a band of people in revolt. He too was killed and all his followers were scattered" (Acts 5:37).

Judas' Disobedience

Judas never submitted his heart to fully follow Jesus as a disciple, but instead, one step of disobedience at a time, was led astray. C.S. Lewis said, "Good and evil increase at compound interest, that's why the little decisions we make every day are of such infinite importance."

John 12:4-6 states, "But one of his disciples, Judas Iscariot, who was later to betray him, objected, 'Why wasn't this perfume sold and the money given to the poor? It was worth a year's wages.' He did not say this because he cared about the poor but because he was a thief (κλεπτης); as keeper of the money bag, he used to help himself to what was put into it."

Judas regularly stole from the offering bag and he lacked the fear of the Lord. His little steps of rebellion led to the moment when he betrayed Jesus to the high priest to be crucified. The first-century rabbis used to say, "All is in the hands of God (external locus) except the fear of God (internal locus)." The gospel writers contrast the woman who poured the expensive perfume on Jesus and her whole-hearted devotions with Judas' betraying and callous heart. They

---

[30] A. Reifenberg, *Israel's History in Coins*. (London: Schocken Books, 1953), 13.

accomplish this comparison by the juxtaposed arrangement of these two events together in the gospel narratives (Mark 14:1-11).

The other disciples deserted Jesus out of fear while Judas betrayed Jesus because his own desires were contrary to Jesus' mission. As a Zealot, Judas was a Zionist rebel who fought against the Roman Empire. He desired a conquest Savior on a white horse, not the suffering servant Messiah, Jesus on a humble donkey. Judas' expectation was a messianic warrior on a white horse with weapons of gold like the one who appeared and fought on behalf of Judas Maccabeus at the battle against Lysias (2 Macc. 11:8).

The chief priests, elders, Sanhedrin, and the crowds, like Judas, desired a conquering Messiah as demonstrated by their command to Pilate to release Barabbas, an insurrectionist, rather than Jesus, the King of the Jews (Mark 15:6-15). Barabbas, like the Zealots, was an accomplice in an uprising against the Roman Empire by committing murder in the rebellion.

Mark and Luke both use the word στασις in reference to Barabbas as one involved in a riot (Mark 15:7, Luke 23:19). John 18:40 refers to Barabbas as a ληστης (bandit), a term that Josephus always employs in connection with Revolutionaries. Robert Eisenman states, "The combinations of the terms "insurrection" and "murder" in the gospels demonstrate that Barabbas was probably a sicarii, a Jewish militant movement that attempted to overthrow the Roman occupiers of their land by force."[31]

Judas' betrayal is insidious by his being one of the twelve apostles who shared in Jesus' ministry, performed miracles, and even expelled demons. He was in the Upper Room next to Jesus at the Last Supper Passover meal, and when Jesus dipped the bread into the bowl with Judas it demonstrated he was in the seat of honor at the meal. The sign that Judas prearranged with the mob was a kiss, and yet when Jesus was betrayed, He addressed Judas as His friend (Matt. 26:49-50).

---

[31] Robert Eisenman, "Gospel Fiction and the Redemonization of Judas." *The Huffington Post*, December 19, 2007.

Judas' Heart

And yet like an insidious disease, undetected by the disciples, Judas left the meal and betrayed Jesus. John 13:2 says, "The evening meal was being served, and the devil had already placed in Judas' heart to betray Jesus." The Greek word in this text βεβληκοτος is a perfect participle and means "placed" or the *NIV* translation "prompted." The basic thought of the perfect tense is that the progress of an action has been completed and the results of that action are continuing on, in full effect in the present.

The devil placed in Judas' heart a desire to betray Jesus and Judas chose to follow that path of betrayal by his actions and deeds. That choice ultimately culminated in his suicide. Professor Henry Ansgar Kelly wrote, "Christ calls Peter the Devil for attempting to avert the Passion and Judas the Devil for working to bring it about. What these two apostles have in common is thrusting their own personal fears into the path of the divine plan of salvation."[32]

Insidious Traps

The devil is only able to tempt us by the desires already in our hearts. James 1:14-15 says, "But each one is tempted when, by his own evil desire, he is dragged away and enticed. Then, after desire has conceived, it gives birth to sin; and sin, when it is full-grown, gives birth to death." Luke 6:45 states, "The good man brings good things out of the good stored up in his heart and the evil man brings evil things out of the evil stored up in his heart." Judas' heart's desire was for a power-yielding Messiah; therefore, Satan was able to deceive him and use him for his own purpose.

Professor Gregory A. Boyd wrote,

> "Hence, a person (Judas) who has solidified his character (*habitus acquires*) as a greedy person by making multitudes of free decisions is morally

---

[32] Henry Ansgar Kelly, "The Devil in the Desert," *Catholic Biblical Quarterly*, 26 (1964), 218.

culpable not only for all the further acts he performs but also and even more fundamentally for being the kind of person he has freely become. Moral culpability is not just about people acting certain ways when they could have and should have acted differently. It's more about people becoming certain kinds of people when they could have and should have become different kinds of people. Hence, if God decides that it fits his providential plan to use a person whose choices have solidified his character as wicked, God is not responsible for this person's wickedness."[33]

Silent Intruders

John 13:27 says, "As soon as Judas took the bread, Satan entered him. 'What you are about to do, do quickly,' Jesus told him." Satan entered Judas quietly with the eleven disciples unaware that the devil was now working in their mist. When the devil and his demons enter an individual they enter him or her silently and undetected, but when they are driven out it is with great force and visibility as with the 2,000 pigs possessed with the legion of demons who rushed down the river bank to their destruction (Mark 5:1-20).

It is just the opposite way in which God and the Holy Spirit enter. When the Holy Spirit entered the believers on the day of Pentecost, there was fire from heaven and the sound of violent wind (Acts 2:1-13). But when the Spirit of God was taken from Samson because of his disobedience, the Spirit left silently and Samson was unaware that God's power had departed (Judges 16:20).

Light & Darkness

John wrote, "As soon as Judas had taken the bread, he went out. And it was night." Night denotes the devil's deception of Judas and

---

[33] Gregory A. Boyd, *Satan and the Problem of Evil* (Downers Grove: InterVarsity Press, 2001), 122.

his blindness to the truth of the light. He was then enslaved to the darkness and confusion. A key motif in John's gospel is the contrast between light and darkness.

Both the disciples and believers are sons of the light and unbelievers are the children of darkness (John 1:5; 3:19-21; 12:35-36). The Pharisee Nicodemus came to Jesus at night, but after he had believed, he went to Pilate in the daylight, and with spices to anoint Jesus' body (John 3:2; 19:38).

Fulfillment of Scriptures

The tripolarity theory, with relationship to Judas' betrayal, demonstrates God is able to transform evil into good and the Father is in complete control. Jesus said, "The Son of Man will go just as it is written about him. But woe to that man who betrays the Son of Man! It would be better for him if he had not been born" (Mark 14:21). The prophets predicted Jesus' passion and Judas' betrayal. Zechariah 11:12-13 says, "I told them, 'If you think it best, give me my pay; but if not, keep it.' So they paid me thirty pieces of silver. And the Lord said to me, 'Throw it to the potter'—the handsome price at which they priced me! So I took the thirty pieces of silver and threw them into the house of the Lord to the potter."

In Psalm 41:9 David also predicted the betrayal: "Even my close friend, whom I trusted, he who shared my bread, has lifted up his heel against me." Matthew, in his gospel account to the Jews, included these two prophesies about Judas to demonstrate that Jesus' passion fulfilled the Old Testament Scriptures.

Judas was unaware he had fulfilled these Scriptures and the death of Jesus brought salvation to the community of believers (Matt. 27:1-10). The four Passion narratives portray Jesus as in complete control of His destiny, even giving commands to His betrayer: "Do it quickly." Jesus said, "Do you think I cannot call on my Father, and he will at once put at my disposal more than twelve legions of angels?" (Matt. 26:53). The Gospel of Luke betrayal narrative adds a miracle. After Jesus' disciple cut off the right ear of the high priest's servant, Jesus said, 'No more of this!' And he touched his ear and healed him (Luke 22:51). In the Gospel of John, the falling of Judas and the soldiers is the natural response to finding a divine being before them (John 18:6).

The gospels portrayed Judas as greedy and crafty by his calculating the exact moment to hand Jesus over to the mob. The irony is that if Judas would have only asked for forgiveness, God would have forgiven him, since the blood of Jesus is able to cleanse all sins (1 John 1:9).

Worldly Sorrow

Matthew records,

> "When Judas, who had betrayed him, saw that Jesus was condemned, he was seized with remorse and returned the thirty silver coins to chief priests and the elders. 'I have sinned,' he said, 'for I have betrayed innocent blood.' 'What is that to us?' they relied. 'That's your responsibility.' So Judas threw the money into the temple and left. Then he went way and hanged himself. The chief priests picked up the coins and said, ' is against the law to put this into the treasury, since it is blood money.' So they decided to use the money to buy the potter's field as a burial place for foreigners. That is why it has been called the Field of Blood to this same day" (Matt. 27:3-8).

Judas felt great grief for betraying Jesus to death and he returned the silver coins to the chief priest and elders. After returning the coins Judas went away and hanged himself. Judas had worldly sorrow that leads to death rather than godly sorrow, which leads to repentance (2 Cor. 7:10).

Divine Irony

Judas in the Hebrew history symbolizes victory, nationalism, and hero. In Christianity the name Judas represents a traitor. The actions and choices of each Judases determine our historic view of them; Maccabeus a hero and godly warrior and Iscariot a traitor and rebel. As King Solomon said, "A good name is more desirable than great riches" (Prov. 22:1).

Professor Neil Forsyth wrote,

> "The irony of the betrayal-crucifixion-resurrection sequence is thus made transparent in the gospel of John. Satan thinks this is his victory, but it is actually the beginning of his defeat. At the moment he enters the human agent Judas, by a demonic inversion of the Eucharistic bread, the opponent himself precipitates the events that are to undo him, moving the plot along to its necessary climax the resurrection."[34]

The final irony with Judas Iscariot is the thing he desired most in life, the overthrow of the Roman Empire and establishment of the Messianic kingdom, Jesus and His followers would accomplish. In 313 A.D., Emperor Constantine and Licinius issued the Edict of Milan legalizing Christian worship and in 380 A.D. Emperor Flavius Theodosius established Christianity as the official religion of Rome. By the end of the fourth century, the majority of Roman citizens had converted to the faith. The Kingdom of God was like a mustard seed and it did not come with a Jewish revolt of swords as Judas had hoped but a wooden cross (Matt. 13:31-32).

Consequences

The devil used Judas to betray Jesus and this led to Judas' own eternal destruction. Acts 1:17-18 says, "He (Judas) was one of our number and shared in this ministry. With the reward he got for his wickedness, he bought a field; there he fell headlong, his body burst open and all his intestines spilled out." The devil's reward for Judas was a violent death. Rick Joyner said, "Satan builds a man up in pride so that he can tear him down and destroy him. The Lord tears a man

---

[34] Neil Forsyth, *The Old Enemy: Satan & the Combat Myth* (Princeton: Princeton University Press, 1987), 316.

down through humility so that He can build him up and use him for His glory."

D.L. Moody said, "The devil is a hard taskmaster." In the tripolarity theory God rewards His faithful servants as Matthew 25:23 states, "His master replied, 'Well done, good and faithful servant! You have been faithful with a few things; I will put you in charge of many things. Come and share your master's happiness!'"

Judas by his choice to rebel was disqualified to receive authority in the kingdom. Jesus promised his twelve apostles, "I tell you the truth, at the renewal of all things, when the Son of Man sits on his glorious throne, you who have followed me will also sit on twelve thrones, and judging the twelve tribes of Israel" (Matt. 19:28).

Luke records in Acts 1:25 when the Church appointed an apostle to take Judas' leadership position the Apostle Peter said, "To take over this apostolic ministry, which Judas left to go where he belongs." The person whom the Church chose to take Judas' ministry was a man with a heart for God name Matthias (Acts 1:24).

Summary

The Scriptures consistently remind us the devil has no power except for what God gives him and what we allow him to exert. Judas' choice to betray Jesus led to his destruction. Job 22:15-16 states, "Will you keep to the old path that evil men have trod? They were carried off before their time, their foundations washed away by a flood." The foundation for the believer is Jesus Christ and He protects us from every attack of the devil (1 Cor. 3:11).

When the devil prowls like a roaring lion or is deceptive as a serpent, God promises to protect us. 1 John 4:4 states, "You, dear children, are from God and have overcome them, because the one who is in you is greater than the one who is in the world."

Chapter 6
Insidious Operation of the Devil: Part 2 (Atheist Madalyn O'Hair)

Hell is the highest reward that the devil can offer to you for being a faithful servant of his.

Evangelist Billy Sunday

God works in mysterious ways;
the devil prowls for his prey in insidious ways.

Ron Sandison

In his pride the wicked does not seek him;
in all his thoughts there is no room for God.

Psalm 10:4

The fool says in his heart, "There is no God."
They are corrupt, their deeds are vile;
there is no one who does good.

Psalm 14:1

Introduction

THE INSIDIOUS OPERATION of the devil is seen by the lurid deaths of atheist Madalyn Murray O'Hair, her son Jon Garth, and granddaughter Robin. In their violent deaths, we can see by faith the tripolarity theory and the devil's destruction, even to his most faithful servant Madalyn. Atheist Madalyn was famous for saying, "There is no God. There's no heaven. There's no hell. There are no angels. When you die, you go in the ground and worms eat you." She was instrumental in removing prayer from public schools with her 1963 Supreme Court lawsuit and was the founder of the American Atheists.

Madalyn preached vehemently, "An atheist believes that a hospital should be built instead of a church. Deeds must be done instead of a prayer said. An atheist strives for involvement in life and not escape into death (internal locus). They want disease conquered, poverty vanished and war eliminated (eternal locus)." As an atheist, Madalyn's locus of control of the universe was only internal, yet the very things she desired most, the end of poverty, disease, and war, can only be accomplished by God, an external source of locus of control (Isaiah 2:4, Micah 4:3, Rev. 21:4). She mocked and blasphemed God by stating, "The real Holy Trinity is anxiety, fear, and guilt." Ironically, the Trinity River would be the clue that solved her murder.

The Flaw of Atheism

If atheism is true, as Madalyn passionately crusaded, then everything is permissible because there is no God to establish and uphold moral absolutes and no golden rule that demand justice. Thus, survival of the fittest becomes the supreme law of the universe and everything is permissible, including murder.

Hell of Violence

On Saturday, January 27, 2001, excavators unearthed the mutilated, hacksawed bodies of atheist Madalyn O'Hair, Jon Garth, and Robin from a shallow grave in the rural Texas Hill Country. Ted Draco author of *Ungodly*, wrote, "Yet the evil revelations held by the grave were not without a dreadful, divine irony, for Madalyn had spent her entire adult life trying to convince the world that only fools believed that there was a Hell."[35] Yet she and her two family

---

[35] Ted Dracos, *Ungodly: The Passions, Torments, and Murder of Atheist Madalyn Murray O'Hair* (New York: Free Press, 2003), 8.

members in their violent deaths experienced real horror and hell on earth. Robin, her granddaughter, was raped and sexually assaulted repeatedly by their captor, Gary Karr. Gary testified, "The murders were conducted so that some family members were still alive and conscious as their loved ones were bludgeoned to death."

Garth's skull was wrapped in a plastic garbage bag and almost the entire circumference of his cranium had tiny hairline fractures. Forensic anthropologist Dr. Glassman summarized his observations crudely stating, "They beat the crap out of Garth repeatedly before he died." Madalyn and Robin most likely were manually strangled according to the forensic report. In their shallow gravesite was the skull of Danny Fry with a bullet hole, along with his decomposed hands. The bodies had a mild charring effect indicating that David Waters and Gary used some flammable substance on their corpses.

One FBI agent at the scene said, "I said a prayer over their bodies; no one deserves this kind of death, no one." Evangelist Bill Murray O'Hair, Madalyn's oldest son, said, "The details of the last days and hours of my mother, brother, and daughter were so brutal that even men accustomed to violence were emotionally shaken."[36]

Natural Born Killer

David Waters, the mastermind behind their nefarious abductions and murders, had spent the majority of his life in prison. He had an IQ in the genius range, but an unstable upbringing and deprived environment contributed to him becoming a murderer and habitual criminal (devil) rather than a successful doctor or lawyer. Betty, his mother, was a stripper and prostitute and her sons were free to roam the neighborhood; they learned from an early age to fend and care for each other. Home for the young Waters was a place where strangers came and went and they had no father figure to guide them in the truth.

---

[36] http://www.crimemagazine.com/murder-madalyn-murray-ohair-americas-most-hated-woman

Professor of psychology Michael S. Zack said, "If you want to scar a child for life use abuse and neglect. Abuse is any action that harms others and neglect is any inaction that causes harm to others." The effects of abuse and neglect can include psychological problems, delay in social development, a tendency to view others as hostile or to be exploited, an inclination for aggression, higher probability to use drugs and alcohol and be involved in self-destructive behaviors and criminal activities.

While David was incarcerated as a young adult, his younger brother Stevie was shot to death. Stevie was high on heroin and confronted his mother with a hammer. When the police demanded that he drop it, he refused. The police shot and killed him in his mother's kitchen and he died at her feet. Betty cruelly said, "If I would have had the gun, I would have shot him myself!" Stevie was David's favorite brother and best friend, and his family failed to notify David in lockup of his death.

Criminal Mind

David's criminal history began on the streets of Peoria, Illinois, a city in the 1950s known for its violence, prostitution, and taverns, and it was the number one distiller in America. As an adolescent, David pushed his youngest brother Jeff into an inferno of burning leaves; the toddler was seriously disfigured. David had no reverence for authority figures and was an antisocial in his respect for the law. At age twelve, he was sent to reform school for theft. David stated upon his release from St. Charles Reform, "I will never again respect authority figures or any retributive measures they might have at their disposal."

Road to Perdition

Missed opportunities contributed to David's road to perdition due to his mother's lack of nurture and love. In 1964 at age seventeen, David desired to be a success and change his life, so he went to a Marine recruiting station. David received a high score on the entrance exam and was recommended for officer candidate school. All that was required for him to join was his mother's signature, since he was four months shy of his eighteenth birthday. But Betty refused to take the time to help her son; a few months later David would choose to get his first taste of blood. Dr. Francis Collins said, "Genetics loads the gun and environment pulls the trigger."

First Blood

On December 13, 1964, David Waters, Robert Duane Taylor, and Carl Welchman were hanging out drinking stolen whiskey, as David Gibbs drove up in his '53 Chevy. The three teenagers had David Gibbs give them a ride into the country and they told him, "We are going to take your car and use it for a drive-by and shoot Jack Lowe!" Gibbs declined and Taylor hit him in the mouth and Welchman hit him in the back. David Waters took control of the wheel while his two friends beat Gibbs unconscious.

As Gibbs's body lay lifeless on the dirt road, David Waters drove Gibbs's Chevy over his legs. Ann Rowe Seaman describes, "Bloody pieces of his shirt and undershirt lay on the side of the road."[37] Two days later the four killers were led to their preliminary hearing and they were spitting and kicking at the news media. The judge generously sentenced them to 30-60 years and they were eligible for parole in only 8 years.

David told his wife, Marti, who was mysteriously murdered in 1980, "The Gibbs murder had nothing to do with drugs or alcohol, it had to do with seeing what it was like to take a life. It was about torture and control." Another ex-girlfriend, Carolyn Bruce, said, "Murder was always on David's mind. He used to tell me, murder is the easiest crime to commit as long as there's no body. In Texas you can hide a body anywhere and it would never be found!"[38] She also described David as the sweetest guy on earth and the most hateful

---

[37] Ann Rowe Seaman, *America's Most Hated Woman* (New York: Continuum Int. Pub., 2005), 96.

[38] Ann Rowe Seaman, *America's Most Hated Woman*, 219.

devil in hell. David was an antisocial personality type and had no conscience about murder. He told another friend, "A victim is someone weak who deserves to be taken advantage of."

Killer on Parole

In August 1976, David Waters, at twenty-nine, was paroled, having spent only twelve years in prison. Less than three years later David was again in trouble with the law for assaulting his mother, Betty. He assaulted her with a broom and broke her ribs and urinated on her face. Again, the judge was merciful to David, and he only sentenced him to a year.

David dreaded contemporary nine-to-five jobs and instead devised schemes to scam money. In 1982, David, at thirty-five, with his girlfriend, twenty-one-year-old Lori, moved to Naples, Florida. About a week later, Billy King's body, covered with bullet marks, was discovered in a van in Peoria; he was one of David's acquaintances. David was the last person King was with alive and yet he was not a suspect in his death. In Naples, David met Danny Fry, a happy-go-lucky man, who had get-rich-quick dreams. Only thirteen years later these dreams would lead to his headless nude corpse being discovered by an elderly man scrounging for aluminum cans by the Trinity River.

Demonic Connection

In August 1985, David went back to jail for fraud; he stole $5,000 using an elderly man's bank account. While in minimum-security Honor Farm in Illinois David met Gary Karr, who had committed rape and robbery and was serving a 30-to-50-year sentence. Eight years later, David and Gary would meet again for an insidious operation. Gary was released from the Honor Farm in April 1995 after serving twenty-one years. A few months later David and he would begin their extortion and murderous operation.

Tragic Demise

On Mother's Day 1980, Madalyn's oldest son, Bill Murray, made Jesus Christ the Lord and Savior of his life and became an evangelist. In response to Bill's conversion Madalyn disowned him. She had forbidden her granddaughter, Robin, to have contact with her dad. Madalyn wrote in her diary, "One could call this a postnatal abortion on the part of a mother, I repudiate Bill entirely and completely for now and all times. He is beyond forgiveness." Bill previously had faithfully served as his mother's office manager for American Atheists.

The *Austin American-Statesman* had an ad that the *Atheist Press* was diligently seeking to hire an office worker with the caption, "Religious persons may feel uncomfortable." In January 1993 Madalyn hired intelligent and charming ex-con David Waters. Little did she know her new employee was the devil, masquerading as a witty, charismatic, ex-con hunk with a criminal record that included four accounts of forgery, assault on his own mother, and cold-blooded murder. As the Scottish proverb states, "The devil's boots don't creak!" Bill speculated his mother hired David Waters for three main reasons: first, as an ex-con she could pay him only seven dollars an hour; second, he would not hesitate to be involved in fraudulent activities; and third, David was a charmer and intellectual type.

Madalyn treated her staff like slaves. She wrote in her personal diary, "We have NO one to work in my offices but scum, chicken f-ckers, fags, masturbators, dumb n-ggers, spicks, derelicts, lumpen proletariat, and transvestites, and I'm supposed to whip them into shape and do something with them."[39]

By the spring of 1994, David had gained the trust of Madalyn and her family and was promoted to office manager. Shortly before his promotion expensive computers were stolen and some valuable bonds removed from the office safe. Madalyn believed that it was done by an inside mole on their staff, yet she had no idea this very

---

[39] Ted Dracos, *Ungodly*, 134.

mole was now her new office manager, David, and she naively entrusted him with the keys and their bank accounts. This decision would haunt them later as Madalyn and her family traveled to California for their lawsuit.

When Madalyn and her family returned from their legal battle with Truth Seeker, an atheist organization founded by James Hervey Johnson in California, they discovered David fired their whole staff, closed the office, and emptied their bank accounts of $54,000. Madalyn was so hated by the community the Austin Police Department refused to investigate the $54,000 in forged checks. Finally, two weeks later, the Austin Police issued a warrant for David Waters's arrest, but failed to place him on their fugitive list.

On July 7, 1994, a whole three months after David Waters was indicted, the Travis County Courts gave David an unbelievable plea-bargain for pleading guilty to theft and three lesser charges. He received ten years' probation, no prison term, and was required to make restitution without any interest. He was given this sentence even though he was a habitual violent criminal and an immediate threat to society. Dracos described this shady plea deal as, "Expunging David's present convictions was like offering underarm deodorant to an angry skunk!"[40]

Perfect Crime

Madalyn, in fear for her family's safety, requested Judge Flowers issue a restraining order for David Waters; the judge declined. In response, Madalyn had a seven-foot chain fence erected around her headquarters and new security codes on her alarms. The nail sealing Madalyn's casket was her retaliation in her atheist partner newsletter of July 1995 ridiculing David Waters. Reporter John MacCormack states this letter lit the fatal spark. Madalyn wrote, "If Mr. Waters had stolen this amount of money from any church, or had invaded the home of a minister, he would have been arrested within hours, tried

---

[40] Ted Dracos, *Ungodly*, 184.

and convicted within days, and would even now be serving a long term in the Texas State penitentiary."

This letter infuriated David and placed in motion his murderous plot. His ex-girlfriend Patty Steffens Chavez told federal authorities in 1999, "After reading this letter, he spoke about seeing Madalyn suffering and snipping off her toes." David, as the former office manager, knew Madalyn had over a million dollars hidden away in overseas accounts and if she disappeared nobody would search for her.

Hidden Wealth

In 1993, Madalyn had continual legal battles with the atheist organization representing James Hervey Johnson's estate and Truth Seeker. These legal conflicts were her own demise caused by her deceitful attempt to seize the Johnson estate at his death. She fraudulently used the Truth Seeker name for donations to her own organizations. Madalyn wrote in her diary, "I have been sued for over a million dollars." In fear her personal lifesavings and organizations' accounts were in jeopardy by this lawsuit, she secretly converted a million dollars of their assets into transferable accounts in New Zealand. This course of action had two ramifications paving their destruction: first, David as her office manager knew they had large amounts of wealth; and second, their staff also knew about the cash and figured Madalyn and her family might mysteriously disappear to New Zealand.

On September 29, 1995, when Madalyn, her son, and granddaughter disappeared, it raised little suspicion among their staff. Ironically only a few months before their disappearance Madalyn was acquitted by Judge Real in the Johnsons' lawsuit and the IRS settled their claim of $1.5 million for only $75,000.

David, infuriated by Madalyn's newsletter and captivated with greed for her vast fortune, plotted to embezzle, kidnap, and murder Madalyn and her family. This violent plot thickened as Waters recruited his former prison buddy Gary Karr and Danny Fry.

Disappearance

On Sunday, August 27, 1995, the O'Hairs went to work as normal, and this marked the final time they were seen by their staff. A few days after the O'Hairs' disappearance, Robin contacted their office and told Ellen Johnson they left for an emergency and to take care of their home and the dogs. Garth talked to Ms. Johnson on twelve different occasions and requested blank checks. In the final conversation Robin had with Ellen, Robin was very distraught and said, "I know you'll do the right thing!"

September 29, 1995, was the last time anyone heard from the three as Jon's cell phone went dead and this foreshadowed the horror about to unfold. In fact, Jon Garth's cell phone records would be the Holy Grail that cracked the cold case.

Held Captive by the Beasts

Madalyn, her son, and granddaughter were held captive for a whole month, while David, Gary, and Danny depleted their accounts. They transferred $600,000 of the stolen O'Hairs' funds into gold coins. During this month, amazingly their captors allowed Garth to travel by himself to transfer money from the American Atheists accounts and receive the gold coins. Garth was truly deceived into believing David and Gary would release his family and him after they received all their funds.

Ann Rowe Seaman, author of *America's Most Hated Woman*, wrote,

> "Waters and Jon Garth would go out shopping and pick up Mexican food and have margaritas. They shared pizza and beer for that month. Waters even bought a video game system for him and Garth and they played for hours. This ticked Madalyn off that

her son was having such fun and joy with their kidnappers."[41]

According to David Waters' account, on Monday, September 25, as he and Garth returned from the local bar to the hotel, when they entered their room, there was dead silence. David stated, "I knew something had gone dead wrong! So I had Garth go into the other room with his mom. As I entered the hotel bedroom, Gary followed me closely behind, and there on the bed was Robin's lifeless body. It was at that moment I knew we had to kill Madalyn and Garth." Danny was traumatized by Robin's death so David and Gary decided he must be eliminated.

Unsolved Mystery

David and Gary, a year after the murders, were in the clear. Just as David had predicted, nobody seemed to care the O'Hairs had vanished. Bill Murray filed a missing persons report, but there was no investigation. The IRS believed the O'Hairs mocked them by not paying the generous $75,000. As the one-year anniversary of the O'Hairs' disappearance approached, the *San Antonio Express-News* editor Fred Bonavita had investigative reporter John MacCormack write an article on the O'Hairs' disappearance.

After MacCormack's first article, he discovered the O'Hairs' disappearance was highly unusual in three main ways: they left their beloved dogs behind; Madalyn had severe diabetes, was dependent on her insulin, and yet it was left in the refrigerator; and their lunch of half-eaten sandwiches was still on the table, as if they departed in a hurry. Also since his initial article the police discovered Robin's Porsche at the airport parking lot and the *Houston Chronicle* in their investigation discovered an ex-cop Mark Sparrow had purchased Garth's beloved Mercedes-Benz for only $15,000 from an impostor. Mark Sparrow with the San Antonio police sketch artist created a

---

[41] Ann Rowe Seaman, *America's Most Hated Woman*, 326.

detailed facial picture of the man from whom he had purchased the Benz, which was aired on *Dateline*.

An atheist staff member tipped MacCormack he should check Madalyn's organization's tax statements, and to his amazement over $625,000 was missing from their tax statement.

A young private investigator, Tim Young, in October offered his services to help MacCormack discover the truth. Jon Garth's phone records led them to discover he had purchased large amounts of gold coins in San Antonio the month of their disappearance. As fate would have it, *Nightline*, ABC's late-evening broadcast, carried MacCormack and Tim Young's investigation of the O'Hairs' disappearance. After the airing of the program, on June 20, 1998, MacCormack received a chilling call from Danny Fry's brother.

Connecting the Dots

Bob Fry recognized from the *Dateline* sketch artist the picture of the man who sold Garth's Benz as an exact match for his brother Danny. He nervously told MacCormack, "My brother Danny has been missing since the end of September 1995, after he had gone to Texas to help David Waters 'set on' some people."[42]

In a subsequent conversation, Bob Fry said Danny had sent him a letter that stated "Don't open until October 3rd." When Bob opened the letter he felt dread descend as he read, "If you're reading this, I'm probably already dead. Take this letter to the FBI." The letter stated David and he were waiting at the Warren Inn for some money and he was assigned the task of watching the O'Hairs. He indicated the events had gone horribly wrong and he was sorry for his involvement, and the FBI would be able to trace this crime back to David Waters. It finished with the words, "These people are animals!"

A few days later, Bob heard a knock on his door and there waiting was Waters and another man. David said, "We were sent

---

[42] Ted Dracos, *Ungodly*, 218.

here to get a letter!" Bob, in fear for his life, pretended he was oblivious his brother had written a letter and asked them where Danny was.

The Final Piece of the Puzzle

The FBI gave little interest in the case until IRS field agent Ed Martin joined the team investigation. MacCormack and Young with their pertinent new evidence in late September had *America's Most Wanted* air the case. Tim Young cunningly sent a traceable gift calling card to David Waters. During the airing of the program David called Gary Karr.

The divine luck cracking this cold case was revealed on October 2, 1998, as MacCormack was surfing the web. An article quickly grabbed his attention: "Nude male corpse found in the Trinity River near Dallas at 2:30 p.m. October 2, 1995. The body was missing hands and head." MacCormack knew it had to be Danny Fry, since the corpse was discovered only a few days after the O'Hairs' abduction in Dallas.

MacCormack contacted Sheriff Robert Bjorklund in charge of the investigation of the Trinity River homicide. He had Bob Fry and other close relatives donate blood for the DNA testing. On January 27, 1999, MacCormack received the long-awaited call from the Dallas County Medical Examiners' office, "The DNA results were the unidentified corpse had a probability of 99.99% was Danny Fry."

This final piece of the puzzle caused the unsolved mystery to unwind and search warrants were issued for David Waters and Gary Karr. On March 24, 1999, the FBI and Dallas sheriff's deputies raided Waters's apartment, discovered ammunition, and arrested him. The nail in the coffin was a picture of David holding a handgun. With this third strike David would spend the rest of his life behind bars. The next day, Karr was charged with a weapons offense as agents seized two loaded handguns from his home. Gary admitted to authorities he and David were involved in the murder of the O'Hairs.

God's Agents

In the midst of the devil's operation God had His redeeming special agents, Bill Murray O'Hair, John MacCormack, Tim Young, IRS investigator Ed Martin, and Bob Fry, who helped bring justice. Bob Fry, in fear for his life and his family's safety, could have chosen to be silent, but instead courageously contacted MacCormack and the authorities. Ironically the FBI and IRS, whom Madalyn and her family hated with a passion, were instrumental in cracking this case.

Bill Murray, the oldest son of Madalyn, demonstrates the tripolarity theory by his glorious conversion in Christ. On the night of January 24, 1980, Bill received Christ as his Lord and Savior. In his book *My Life without God*, Bill gives his personal testimony from the grip of the devil to the grace of Christ.[43] Bill testified after his conversion God was no longer a distant force, but a personal friend.

The Devil

Madalyn's death demonstrates in the tripolarity theory the devil's purpose for humanity is destruction. As John 10:10 says, "The thief (devil) comes only to steal and to kill and destroy; I have come that they may have life, and have it to the full."

David Waters in 1997 with ghostwriter Harry Preston wrote a book entitled *Code Name Satan* on the O'Hairs' disappearance and that they absconded to New Zealand or Mexico with atheist funds. "*Code Name Satan*," David's book, demonstrates the devil is the father of lies, since David himself had killed the O'Hairs (John 8:44).

Choice

David Waters, Gary Karr, and Danny Fry all chose by their free will to exhort and kidnap Madalyn and her family and the devil used their decisions for his operation. Madalyn chose to hire ex-convicts to save money and this choice contributed to her death. Bill Murray

---

[43] William J. Murray, *My Life without God* (Eugene: Harvest House, 1992), 300-301.

chose to follow Christ; this decision has brought him out of the darkness.

One of the teens involved with David Waters in the 1964 murder of David Gibbs became a Christian and he witnessed to David about Christ's love and grace. Imagine how different David's life might have become if he would have chosen to follow Christ.

God

Finally, God is the one who brings about justice and divine retribution and He foils the devil's plans. Ironically, the very evidence that solved the O'Hairs' murder case was the discovery of the body of Danny Fry in the Trinity River.

Divine retribution is demonstrated by the $600,000 in gold coins locked in a public storage unit rented by David Waters and Gary Karr that three teens randomly broke in and stole the 120 pounds of gold. By the time the FBI caught up with these teens four years later they spent all the gold on strip clubs and drugs. FBI spokesman Roderick Beverly said, "We believe they discovered the coins by accident; it was just dumb luck."

Summary

The operation of the devil led to a path of destruction for Madalyn, Jon Garth, Robin, David Waters, Gary Karr, and Danny Fry. As Numbers 32:23 states, "You may be sure that your sin will find you out." David Waters received his sentence for Conspiracy to Interfere with Commerce by Robbery and Extortion on January 24, 2001. He was 54, and would serve twenty years with no chance of parole, in addition to another eight years without parole, plus sixty state years, served consecutively.[44] David Waters died in Federal Medical Center in Butner, North Carolina, in spring 2003 of lung cancer.

---

[44] Ann Rowe Seaman, *America's Most Hated Woman*, 319.

Gary Karr in mid-August 2000, was sentenced to two life terms and two ten-year terms, with no parole; he is currently serving his sentence in a federal prison in Florida.

Madalyn and Jon Garth and Robin O'Hairs' remains were buried by her son Bill Murray in an undisclosed location.

Ted Dracos in *Ungodly* summarizes the circumstances of loci of control leading to the discovery of the O'Hairs' corpses and the arrest of David and Gary:

> "It would take an extraordinary set of circumstances to effect justice—a set of circumstances perhaps beyond conventional probabilities. If a veteran newspaper reporter hadn't become mesmerized by a long-shot story and been surfing wire copy on Oct. 2, 1998, at precisely the right moment; and if a young but extremely able private investigator hadn't offered his services at a propitious time; and if a network news correspondent hadn't come up with the idea of a composite sketch, and had it executed by a skilled artist, and the brother of the victim hadn't been watching *Dateline*; and if three amateur punks hadn't been ripping off storage lockers with the precise skeleton key at the perfect place and time; and if three top-of-their game law enforcement agents hadn't confederated their individual talents—David Waters and Gary Karr would have been free."[45]

---

[45] Ted Dracos, *Ungodly*, 266-267.

Chapter 7
Perception and Choice

The root determines the fruit;
choices determine the destination.

Ron Sandison

Choices in life may seem easy at the time, but the
consequences are the hard part because we are forced to live
with them.

Ron Sandison

But if serving the Lord seems undesirable to you, then
choose for yourselves this day whom you will serve,
whether the gods your forefathers served beyond the river,
or the gods of the Amorites, in whose land you are living.
But as for me and my household, we will serve the Lord.

Joshua 24:15

For many are called, but few are chosen.

Matthew 22:14

Introduction

"FATHER TERAH HAD MANY SONS, many sons had Father Terah. I am one of them and so are you, so let's just praise the Lord. Right arm, left arm, right foot, left foot, chin up, turn around!" In Sunday school classes we will never hear this version of the song "Father Abraham" because Terah, the Father of Abraham, unlike his son chose not to go when God called him but settled in Haran.

Genesis 11:31 states, "Terah took his son Abram, his grandson Lot son of Haran, and his daughter-in-law Sarai, the wife of his son Abram, and together they set out from Ur of the Chaldeans to go to Canaan. But when they came to Haran, they settled there."

Terah with his whole family set out on a journey to Canaan which is known as the Promised Land, a region of rich soil. Along the journey, Terah chose to settle in Haran. Terah's decision to settle resulted in him being forgotten in the annals of history and not a founder of a great nation. Moses, the author of Genesis, connects Terah and the Table of Nations with the Tower of Babel narrative with the word "settle." The Tower of Babel narrative begins with the people on earth settling eastward at a plain in Shinar (Gen. 11:1). This settling, instead of subduing the earth and the people building a ziggurat into the heavens, resulted in God scattering the inhabitants of the earth and confusing their languages (Gen. 11:9).

After the dispersion of the nations and the dividing of the continents, God commanded Abraham to go. The Lord told Abraham, "Leave your country, your people, and your father's household and go to the land I will show you. I will make you into a great nation and I will bless you" (Gen. 12:1-2). Abraham was obedient and went as God commanded him; he became the father of a great nation Israel. He is the Jewish and Christian model of faith and was called in Scriptures a friend of God. Terah is remembered only as the father of Abraham.

What caused Abraham to be obedient and go, and Terah to settle? Abraham and Terah by their decisions demonstrate the power of perception and choice in the tripolarity theory and its impact on our destinies. Abraham believed God and it was credited to him as righteousness and Terah settled at Haran and died there.

We can only speculate the reasons Terah decided to settle in Haran. Maybe Terah perceived Haran as a safe region for his family or he became complacent and had no desire to endure an intense journey in the desert being over seventy years old. He may have experienced fear at the prospect of traveling to a foreign land. After all, the city Terah settled was named in honor of his own son Haran.

Perception & Choice

Our perception and beliefs influence our choices and decisions. Abraham, unlike his father, Terah, was quick to obey God. When God commanded Abraham to sacrifice his promised son Isaac on Mount Moriah, Abraham arose early in the morning (Gen. 22:3). And Abraham instructed his servants, "Stay here with the donkeys while I and the boy go over there. We will worship and then we will come back to you" (Gen. 22:5). Abraham believed God was able to fulfill His promise and would protect his son. This faith in God's goodness caused Abraham to choose to obey God. Oswald Chambers wrote, "The great point of Abraham's faith in God was that he was prepared to do anything for God. He was there to obey God, no matter to what belief He went contrary."[46]

Abraham's obedience gave him a greater revelation of the nature of God as God provided a ram in the thicket for his sacrifice. He learned by his experience that God is his provider. Genesis 22:14 says, "So Abraham called that place The Lord Will Provide. And to this day it is said, "On the mountain of the Lord it will be provided." This event foreshadowed the Father offering Jesus His only Son on an altar, the cross.

Hebrews 11:8-10 gives a detailed record of Abraham's perception and faith:

> "By faith Abraham, when called to go to a place he would later receive as his inheritance, obeyed and went, even though he did not know where he was going. By faith he made his home in the promised land like a stranger in a foreign county; he lived in tents, as did Isaac and Jacob, who were heirs with him

---

[46] Oswald Chambers, *My Utmost for His Highest* (Uhrichsville: Barbour Publishing, 1935), entry April 26.

of the same promise. For he was looking forward to the city with foundations, whose architect and builder is God."

Abraham's faith in God caused him to be obedient. He believed God as the Creator was able to raise Isaac from death and he could trust God to lead him. Outward appearance and circumstances like Sarah's barrenness did not dictate Abraham's perception of God and His ability to fulfill the promise. Romans 4:18-22 says,

"Against hope, Abraham in hope believed and so became the father of many nations, just as it had been said to him, 'So shall your offspring be.' Without weakening in his faith, he faced the fact that his body was as good as dead—since he was about a hundred years old—and that Sarah's womb was also dead. Yet he did not waver through unbelief regarding the promise of God, but was strengthened in his faith and gave glory to God, being fully persuaded that God had power to do what he had promised. This is why "it was credited to him as righteousness.'"

Abraham's faith produced corresponding actions and good works. As James wrote,

"You foolish man, do you want evidence that faith without deeds is dead? Was not our ancestor Abraham considered righteous for what he did when he offered his son Isaac on the altar? You see that his faith and his actions were working together, and his faith was made complete by what he did" (James 2:20-22).

In the tripolarity theory with regard to perception and choice, we need to believe God is good (perception) and we must decide to obey His commands (choice) because His commands are based on His unfailing love. Our faith, like Abraham's, must have corresponding good works. John Bevere said, "Disobedience communicates to those around us that we know more than God."

Faith in the guidance of God causes us to follow Him in obedience. If our perception is perverted this will hinder us from fulfilling the will of God. We will become deceived and double minded and not trust God.

Proverbs 3:5-6 states, "Trust in the Lord with all your heart and lean not on your own understanding; in all your ways acknowledge him and he will make your paths straight." One variant of Proverbs 3:6 texts translates, "He will direct your paths." The Reformer John Calvin said, "Understanding is born out of obedience to God." As we follow God wholeheartedly then He directs our paths and makes them straight.

Perverted

Our perception becomes perverted by disobedience. When we know God's will and choose to disobey them, we become deceived and darkened in our spiritual understanding. Sin distorts our perception of the voice of God, the character of God, and our relationship with God. We may believe we are serving God while we are really serving our own carnal desires. The Apostle James wrote,

> "Do not merely listen to the word, and so deceive yourselves. Do what it says. Anyone who listens to the word but does not do what it says is like a man who looks at his face in a mirror and, after looking at himself, goes away and immediately forgets what he looks like" (James 1:22-24).

Our choices shape our perception of God. If we study God's Word and do not obey it, we will become deceived and our perceptions of God will be distorted. Romans 1:21-25 describes the depraved mind:

> "For although they knew God, they neither glorified him as God nor gave thanks to him, but their thinking

became futile and their foolish hearts were darkened. Although they claimed to be wise, they became fools and exchanged the glory of the immortal God for images made to look like mortal man and birds and animals and reptiles. Therefore God gave them over in the sinful desires of their hearts to sexual impurity for the degrading of their bodies with one another. They exchanged the truth of God for a lie, and worshipped and served created things rather than the Creator—who is forever praised. Amen."

The Gentiles' disobedience to the innate truth of God in their conscience caused them to be distorted in their perception of the character of the Creator, and to portray Him in the form of idols. They formed God into their own likeness and perceived the Creator to be a glorified image of themselves. This pseudo-perception made their minds become depraved and only able to choose to follow their unrestrained appetites. They were enslaved to their base urges and unable to perceive God's truth in creation and worship the Creator. This deception of the mind paves the path to demonic influence.

The Apostle Paul warns believers, "The Spirit clearly says that in later times some will abandon the faith and follow deceiving spirit things taught by demons. Such teachings come through hypocritical liars, whose consciences have been seared with a hot iron" (1 Tim.4:1-2). A seared conscience causes an individual to be unable to distinguish between truth and falsehood, good and evil, God and the demonic. As touching a hot iron for an extended period of time with the palm of your hand would result in severe nerve damage to tissue cells and make you cease to sense pain, a seared conscience makes you unable to perceive God and causes you to be open to demonic deception.

An example of demonic deception in the name of God is John List, a Lutheran who in 1971 with a seared conscience murdered his mother, wife, daughter, and two sons. John, for months leading up to the murder of his family, had contemplated their murders. He was so deceived in his mind and seared in his conscience he perceived their murders to be the permissive will of God. After the murders, John wrote this letter of justification to his pastor, Eugene Rehwinkel:

"I am very sorry to add this additional burden to your work. I know that what has been done is wrong from all that I have been taught and that any reasons that I might give will not make it right. But you are the one person that I know that while not condoning this will at least possibly understand why I felt that I had to do this.

1. I wasn't earning anywhere near enough to support us. Everything I tried seemed to fall to pieces. True, we could have gone bankrupt & maybe gone on welfare.

2. But that brings me to my next point. Knowing the type of location that one would have to live in plus the environment for the children plus the effect of them knowing they were on welfare was just more than I thought they could and should endure. I know that they were willing to cut back but this involved a lot more than that.

3. With Pat (daughter) being so determined to get into acting, I was also fearful as to what this might do to her continuing to be a Christian. I'm sure it wouldn't have helped.

4. Also with Helen (wife) not going to church, I know that this would harm the children eventually in their attendance. I had continued to hope that she would begin to come to church soon . . ."

John List concludes his demonic and self-justification letter stating,

"Originally, I had planned this for Nov. 1—All Saints Day. But travel arrangements were delayed. I thought it would be an appropriate day for them to get to heaven. As for me, please let me be dropped from the congregation rolls. I leave myself in the hands of God's justice & mercy. I don't doubt that He is able to help us, but apparently He saw fit not to answer my prayers the way I had hoped they would be answered. This makes me think (perception) that perhaps it was for the best as far as the children's souls are concerned. I know that many will only look at the additional years that they could have lived, but if finally they were no longer Christians, what would be gained . . .

Please remember me in your prayers. I will need them whether or not the government does its duty as it sees it. I'm only concerned with making my peace with God and of this I am assured because Christ died even for me.

P.S. Mother is in the hallway in the attic—third floor. She was too heavy to move. "

John [47]

John List's mind had become so deceived and seared that he perceived murdering his family was his only rational option. He even blamed God in his letter for his act, stating, "God did not answer my prayers as I had hoped." John perceived his situation as beyond God's control.[48]

In his hopeless perception and psychopathic state of mind, John chose to murder his family and the devil deceived him to believe this was God's permissive will because his family would now be safe in

---

[47] John Walsh with Philip Lerman, *No Mercy* (New York: Pocket Books, 1998), 73-75.

[48] See endnotes: John List's explanation for murdering his family.

heaven. John Lehrer, author of *How We Decide* describes the psychopathic mind:

> "The rational brain can explain the verdict for our every decision and justify them. It provides reasons, but those reasons all come after the fact. This is why psychopaths are so dangerous: they are missing the emotions (conscience) that guide moral decisions in the first place. There's a dangerous void where their feelings are supposed to be. For people like John Gacy, sin is always intellectual, never visceral. As a result, a psychopath is left with nothing but a rational lawyer inside his head, willing to justify any action. Psychopaths commit violent crimes because their emotions (conscience) never tell them not to."[49]

John List's twisted perception caused him to view himself as an instrument and savior of his family's redemption rather than the truth, a cold-blooded murderer. A year after the murders, John was still a fugitive of the law and the home where the murders occurred in New Jersey mysteriously burned down. In Tim Benford's book *Righteous Carnage*, Tim mentions the divine irony of what the man who bought John's house discovered after the fire.

This fire revealed a hidden treasure; the enormous stained-glass ceiling in the ballroom was signed by Louis Comfort Tiffany. In 1971, these windows would have been valued at over $100,000. Tim states, "Had John List only turned his eyes to heaven before the murders, and seen what was actually in front of him instead of what he perceived, his problems would have been solved." John's pseudo-perception and deception caused him to make deadly choices. On June 1, 1989, John List, a fugitive of the law for nearly 18 years, was captured thanks to *America's Most Wanted*. He was sentenced to life without parole and at age 82 on March 21, 2008, died of pneumonia alone in prison.

---

[49] John Lehrer, *How We Decide* (New York: Mariner Books, 2009), 175.

How different John's life could have been if only he had seen his circumstances from a divine perspective rather than a hopelessness complex. If John would have just trusted God and persevered in faith, the fire would have revealed God's provision. The Reformer John Calvin said, "Don't tell God how big your mountain is, but instead tell your mountain how big your God is!" Obedience and pure motives protect us from demonic influence. Ananias and Sapphira demonstrated the tripolarity theory and deception by impure motives.

Ananias & Sapphira

Luke records,

> "Joseph, a Levite from Cyprus, whom the apostle called Barnabas (which means "Son of Encouragement"), sold a field he owned and brought the money and put it at the apostles' feet. Now a man named Ananias, together with his wife Sapphira, also sold a piece of property. With his wife's full knowledge he kept back part of the money for himself, but brought the rest and put it at the apostles' feet.
>
> Then Peter said, "Ananias, how is it that Satan has so filled your heart that you have lied to the Holy Spirit and have kept for yourself some of the money you received for the land? Didn't it belong to you before it was sold? And after it was sold, wasn't the money at your disposal? What made you think of doing such a thing? You have not lied to men but to God." When Ananias heard this, he fell down and died. And great fear seized all who heard what had happened" (Acts 4:36; 5:1-5).

Barnabas sold one of his fields and donated the whole amount of money to the believers. This generous act of Barnabas helped the poor in the church and caused him to have a reputation as an encourager. Ananias and his wife, Sapphira, coveting the praise the believers gave to Barnabas, decided to sell a piece of property. Unlike Barnabas, who gave sacrificially, they chose to hold a portion of the money back and falsely portray they had given the whole amount. Peter, by the discernment of the Holy Spirit, revealed their deception and pronounced God's judgment. The judgment was severe and swift and Ananias and Sapphira were struck dead. Why was God's judgment swift and severe for their sin of disobedience?

In the Scriptures the greater the manifestation of God's presence, the swifter the divine judgment. Prior to this event in Acts 4:31 Luke records, "After they prayed, the place where they were meeting was shaken. And they were filled with the Holy Spirit and spoke the word of God boldly." The manifested presence of God was powerful in the early church and this caused God's judgment to be swift and an abundance of miracles (Acts 5:12-16).

When the boy Samuel ministered in the temple under Eli, the presence of God was rare and His judgment was delayed (1 Sam. 3:1). Eli's sons Hophni and Phinehas were priests with wicked hearts and darkened consciences; they had sex with the women who served at the entrance to the Tent of Meeting and treated the Lord's offering with contempt holding back the best portions of the sacrifice (1 Sam. 2:12-17; 2:22-25).

It is interesting to note that the new temple of God is the community of believers, so Ananias and Sapphira holding back the portion is equivalent to Eli's sons holding back part of the sacrifice. Before God brought judgment on Hophni and Phinehas, He sent a prophet to rebuke Eli for his sons' wicked deeds (1 Sam. 2:27-36).

When the Ark of God was captured by the Philistines and 30,000 Israelite foot soldiers were slaughtered, both Eli's sons were killed on the same day. God's judgment was not swift like with the High priest Aaron's sons Nadab and Abihu because the presence of the Lord was rare and there were not many miracles.

When Aaron, the brother of Moses, was high priest, the presence of the Lord filled the Tabernacle and fire from heaven devoured the sacrifices. Aaron's sons in the manifested presence of God chose to offer unauthorized fire and they were consumed immediately by God's wrath (Lev. 10:1-3). Judgment was immediate because the presence of God was tangible.

The tripolarity theory is seen in the narrative of Ananias and Sapphira by their choice to hold back some of the money and lie to the church (human agent/free will), Satan deceiving them to be dishonest (devil agent/evil) and the Holy Spirit revealing their sin and bringing judgment (divine agent). Ananias and Sapphira perceived that God was unable to supply all their needs and this caused them to hold back a portion of the money. This act of disobedience resulted in them being deceived by Satan and receiving God's wrath.

Perception & Choice

A divine perception in the tripolarity theory is to believe by faith that God is our source of life. Since God is supreme we must be quick like Abraham to obey His commands. Isaiah 66:2 states, "Has not my hand made all these things, and so they came into being?" Declares the Lord, "This is the one I esteem: he who is humble and contrite in spirit, and trembles at my word." When we revere and respect God then He reveals Himself to us through His Word (Ps. 25:14).

We need to tremble at God's Word and when we hear His voice be quick to respond in obedience. John Bevere said, "Obedience is the highest form of worship." As Abraham journeyed to Mount Moriah to offer his son Isaac as a sacrifice, he told his servants, "I and the boy are going up to the mount to worship" (Gen. 22:5). Obedience demands we put our desires to death in order to serve God and others.

Perception determines the choices we make either to obey God or be disobedient. Do we view our circumstances from God's eternal perspective or from our limited knowledge? How do we see those around us? As people created in the image of God or as a nuisance?

Perception & People

Martin Luther said, "God doesn't need our good works, but our neighbor does." Our perception of others determines the way we choose to treat and love them. Jesus taught that the way we treat others is the manner we treat Him. Matthew 25:37-41:

> "Then the righteous will answer him, 'Lord, when did we see you hungry and feed you, or thirsty and give you something to drink? When did we see you a stranger and invite you in, or needing clothes and clothe you? When did we see you sick or in prison and go to visit you?'

> The King will reply, 'I tell you the truth, whatever you did for one of the least of these brothers of mine, you did for me.' Then he will say to those on his left, 'Depart from me, you who are cursed, into the eternal fire prepared for the devil and his angels.'"

In this parable on the judgment seat of Christ, we are judged by the way we treated others. Those who spend eternity with Christ cared for the outcast; those who are thrown into hell decided to ignore their desperate plea. This text implies that there will be some other sheep (people of different theologies) who will enter the kingdom unaware, as they helped the needy and outcasts, they were doing it for Jesus.

Jesus said, "I have other sheep that are not of this sheep pen. I must bring them also. They too will listen to my voice, and there shall be one flock and one shepherd" (John 10:16). When the disciples rebuked a man who was driving out demons in the name of Jesus, who was not part of their tight community, Jesus exhorted them, "Whoever is not against us is for us. I tell you the truth, anyone who gives you a cup of water in my name because you belong to Christ will certainly not lose his reward" (Mark 10:40-41). There will be people in heaven who gave cold water to the needy and helped God's children with love whose theology was unorthodox and were not a part of our exclusive community.

Our perception of people determines the way we choose to treat them. Do we view people as Jesus and worthy of our love? The only man-made things in heaven are the scars in Jesus' wrists, ankles, and side. Jesus' scars demonstrate the Father's love for us and everyone He created.

Angels

As we choose to serve people, then God reveals Himself. The writer of Hebrews said, "Do not forget to entertain strangers, for by so doing some people have entertained angels without knowing it" (Heb. 13:2). We need to believe that God and His angels are present in the world and choose to be sensitive to the Holy Spirit. An angel or messenger from God may come to us in the form of a friend encouraging us in a season of suffering or an actual angel protecting us from a natural disaster.

Luke 22:23-24 records, "An angel from heaven appeared to Jesus and strengthened him. And being in anguish, he prayed more earnestly, and his sweat was like drops of blood falling to the ground." As Jesus prayed, an angel strengthened Him and gave Him power to endure the cross. We as children of God have angels that work on our behalf. Hebrews 1:14 states, "Are not all angels ministering spirits sent to serve those who will inherit salvation?"

Destiny

Our perception determines our choices and the type of fruit we bear. Abraham believed God, was obedient to Him, and he received the promised son, Isaac. Genesis 24:1 states, "Abraham was now old and well advanced in years, and the Lord had blessed him in every way." Terah chose to stay in the comfort of Haran and missed entering the Promised Land.

As we perceive God loves us, we realize we have a purpose. We are able to enjoy life and be creative with hope for the future. James Michener, author of *Tales of the South Pacific*, wrote in his autobiography,

> "The master in the art of living makes little distinction between his work and play, his labor and his leisure, his mind and his body, his information and his recreation, his love and his religion. He hardly knows which is which. He simply pursues his vision of excellence at whatever he does, leaving others to decide whether he is working or playing. To him, he's always doing both."[50]

The art of living for the believer is whatever we choose to do, we do for the glory of Christ. Colossians 3:17 says, "And whatever you do, whether word or deed, do it all in the name of the Lord Jesus, giving thanks to God the Father through him."

Summary

The choices we make in life based on our perceptions determine whether we fulfill God's purpose. Pastor Jack Hayford said, "If you are surrendered to the will of God, you can't miss it." God's leading will protect us from demonic deception and give us a heart that hears the Master's voice and chooses to obey.

---

[50] Stuart Brown, M.D., with Christopher Vaughan, *Play* (New York: Penguin Group, 2009), 155.

Chapter 8
Growth

Observe a tree, how it first tends downwards, that it may then shoot forth upwards. It fastens its root low in the ground, that it may send forth its top towards heaven. Is it not from humility that it endeavors to rise? But without humility it will not attain to higher things. We desire to grow up into the air without a root. Such is not growth and maturity, but collapse and destruction.

St. Augustine

If my life is fruitless, it doesn't matter who praises me, and if my life is fruitful, it doesn't matter who criticizes me.

John Bunyan

Instead, speaking the truth in love, we will in all things grow up into him who is the Head, that is, Christ. From him the whole body, joined and held together by every supporting ligament, grows and builds itself up in love, as each part does its work.

Ephesians 4:15-16

And not hold fast to the Head, from whom the whole body, nourished and held together by its joints and ligaments, grows with a growth that is from God.

Colossians 2:19

Introduction

DURING FINALS WEEK, my roommate Wes and I went to a movie on a Friday night. As we drove back to our dorm, we saw a rusty 1986 Calais Oldsmobile with a golden crown air freshener on the dashboard and fluorescent purple lights underneath. We simultaneously chuckled and exclaimed, "Now that's ghetto!" I grinned and said to Wes, "What's the meaning of ghetto?" As we went to sleep we discussed the meaning of ghetto. By daybreak we agreed on a definition: "Ghetto is the continual process of doing something counterproductive over an extended period of time."

Ghetto is the apex vise hindering our spiritual growth; the continual process of counterproductive behaviors or activities. Maturity is the opposite of ghetto: "Our capacity to undergo continual transformation in order to adapt successfully and cope flexibly with the demands and responsibilities of life."

Pastor Mike Slaughter wrote, "Fruitfulness is the consequence of obedient persistence in the same direction for the duration of a lifetime."[51] English novelist Charles Reade describes this obedient persistence in his famous statement, "Sow a thought, and you will reap an act; sow an act, and you will reap a habit; sow a habit, and you will reap a character; sow a character, and you will reap a destiny."

Oswald Chambers said, "The great hindrance in spiritual growth is that we will look for big things to do. We tend to forget that Jesus took a towel and began to wash the disciples' feet. There are times when there is no illumination and no thrill, but just the daily round, the common tasks of life. These bring true spiritual growth."

Source of Growth

Spiritual growth in the tripolarity theory is accomplished by choosing to follow Christ daily and allowing Him to transform our lives. 2 Corinthians 3:18 says, "And we, who with unveiled faces all

---

[51] Mike Slaughter, *Change the World* (Nashville: Abingdon Press, 2010), 105.

reflect the Lord's glory, are being transformed into his likeness with ever-increasing glory, which comes from the Lord, who is the Spirit." The Greek word "transform," in this text μεταμορφουμεθα, means "an outward change from an inward transformation," such as a caterpillar turning into a butterfly. This word is a divine passive demonstrating God is the source of our transformation.

Fruitfulness

St. Augustine said, "Merely existing without yielding fruit is not the purpose for which human beings are given the gift of life." John 15:8 states, "This is to my Father's glory, that you bear much fruit, showing yourselves to be my disciples." Our fruits demonstrate to the world Christ has transformed our lives. The power to produce fruit is both external (God) and internal (choice/human agents). Jesus said, "I am the vine; you are the branches. If a man remains in me and I in him, he will bear much fruit; apart from me you can do nothing" (John 15:5). The Holy Spirit empowers us to produce fruit: "But the fruit of the Spirit is love, joy, peace, patience, kindness, goodness, faithfulness, gentleness, and self-control" (Gal. 5:22-23).

The internal power to mature is our decision to make right choices and the encouragement of our brothers and sisters in Christ. Solomon said, "As iron sharpens iron, so one man sharpens another" (Prov. 27:17). Proverbs 13:20 states, "He who walks with the wise grows wise, but a companion of fools suffers harm." My dad says, "If you hang around with junkyard dogs—don't be surprised if you get fleas." The Apostle Paul said, "Do not be misled! Bad company corrupts good character. Come back to your senses as you ought, and stop sinning; for there are some who are ignorant of God—I say this to your shame'" (1 Cor. 15:33).

New Heart

Spiritual growth requires external and internal locus of control— God's power and our surrender to Him. When we receive Jesus as our Lord and Savior, we are born again and receive a new heart and the Holy Spirit abides in us. Jeremiah 36:26-27 says, "I will give you a new heart and put a new spirit in you; I will remove from you your heart of stone and give you a heart of flesh. And I will put my Spirit in you and move you to follow my decrees and be careful to keep my laws."

The Holy Spirit and new heart creates in us a desire to serve Christ. Spiritual growth is living by the power of the Holy Spirit and allowing Him to transform our lives. The Apostle Paul wrote, "Therefore, I urge you, brothers, in view of God's mercy, to offer your bodies as living sacrifices, holy and pleasing to God—this is your spiritual act of worship. Do not conform any longer to the pattern of this world, but be transformed by the renewing of your mind. Then you will be able to test and approve what God's will is— his good pleasing and perfect will" (Rom. 12:1-2).

Renewing Our Minds

Spiritual growth occurs as we offer our bodies as living sacrifices to God and renew our minds by the word of God. D.L. Moody had written on the inside of his personal Bible, "The Bible will keep you from sin or sin will keep you from the Bible." Moody preached, "The Bible was not given only to increase our knowledge but to transform our lives." We renew our minds by reading God's word daily and obeying His word. As we read the Scriptures, the Holy Spirit teaches us how to apply God's word to our lives; He causes certain verses to speak directly to our situations. Jesus said, "But the Counselor, the Holy Spirit, whom the Father will send in my name, will teach you all things and will remind you of everything I have said to you" (John 14:26).

Our minds were not instantly transformed as we received Christ as our Lord but still have some of the previous mindsets that are contrary to God's will. Theses mindsets are transformed and conformed to God's will as we follow the Spirit. The new heart, being born again, causes us to have a desire to obey God. Our previous mindsets, "flesh," can lead us astray into sin. The devil leads us astray by deceiving our minds not to believe the truths in God's word.

Mindsets

One of the main destructive mindsets the devil uses to hinder spiritual growth is to pervert our view of self-efficacy (internal locus) and divine-efficacy (external locus). Self-efficacy is the belief that one has the competence and ability to accomplish their goals.[52] Ten of the twelve spies Moses sent to explore the paradisiacal land had this lack of healthy self-efficacy mindset and reported, "We looked like grasshoppers compared to them and are unable to take the land!" (Numbers 13). Joshua and Caleb had divine and self-efficacy from their renewed minds and said, "We should go up and take possession of the land, for we can certainly do it" (Numbers 13:30). This self-efficacy with the divine caused them to be the only two in their generation to enter the Promised Land. Numbers 14:24 states, "But because my servant Caleb has a different spirit and follows me wholeheartedly, I will bring him into the land he went to, and his descendants will inherit it."

The devil perverts our self-efficacy with thoughts of guilt, insecurity and pride. He attempts to create strongholds in our minds that we are unworthy to be used by God or incompetent to ever conquer our sins. These false ideas veil us from experiencing God's grace and freedom and result in self-defeat. If we succeed in conquering a sin with this perverted mindset, we have the vice of pride and failure to overcome results in the feeling of guilt. When we have self-efficacy and divine-efficacy we have faith and confidence—God is able to use us.

John Bevere wrote, "It takes genuine humility to have faith, because when you are humble you rely on and trust in God's ability (grace) to pull you through—not on your own ability. If the ten spies

---

[52] See endnotes: Self-determination.

had humbly relied on God's promises, they would have moved out and conquered the land."[53]

Divine-efficacy is the belief God is competent to fulfill His promises and empower us for ministry. 2 Corinthians 3:4-6 describes healthy divine-efficacy and says, "Such confidence as this is ours through Christ before God. Not that we are competent in ourselves to claim anything for ourselves, but our competence comes from God. He has made us competent as ministers of a new covenant—not of the letter but of the Spirit; for the letter kills, but the Spirit gives life."

Divine-efficacy has confidence God will fulfill His call on our lives. Philippians 1:6 states, "Being confident of this, that he who began a good work in you will carry it on to completion until the day of Christ Jesus." 1 Thessalonians 5:24 says, "The one who calls you is faithful and he will do it." The divine-efficacy mindset is the faith of the Prophet Daniel's friends who trusted God in the midst of uncertainty without presumptions. Daniel 3:17-18 states, "If we are thrown into the blazing furnace, the God we serve is able to save us from it, and he will rescue us from your hand, O king. But even if he does not, we want you to know, O king that we will not serve your gods or worship the image of gold that you have set up."

Self-efficacy without divine-efficacy can lead to pride: "I did it all by myself." Divine-efficacy alone can cause false presumptions: "God will accomplish it by Himself and I don't need to do anything." This divine-efficacy-only mindset can hinder us from taking the necessary steps of obedience to be prepared for the increase.

These strongholds are destroyed by taking the devil's false ideas captive and renewing our minds by the Scriptures. The Apostle Paul wrote of this battle of the mind and said,

> "For though we live in the world, we do not wage
> wars as the world does. The weapons we fight with

---

[53] John Bevere, *Relentless* (Colorado Springs: WaterBrook Press, 2011), 125-126.

are not the weapons of the world. On the contrary, they have divine power to demolish strongholds. We demolish arguments and every pretension that sets itself up against the knowledge of God, and we take captive every thought to make it obedient to Christ" (2 Cor. 10:3-5).

Types of Growth

The three main types of growth humans experience are physical/biological, knowledge, and spiritual. Physical/biological growth occurs over a period of time by the process of childhood development. An infant eats and receives nourishment and this causes them to grow physically. This form of growth is by linear time plus nourishment. As British writer Tom Stoppard said, "I think age is a very high price to pay for maturity." The second type of growth, knowledge, comes by time plus study. As we study we grow in knowledge and gain a greater understanding of life. Spiritual growth is not achieved by time, study, or knowledge, but only by obedience to God. Thomas A. Kempis said, "One step forward in obedience is worth more than a lifetime study about it."

An individual could be a Christian for years and still be an infant in diapers if they choose to be disobedient to Christ. 1 Corinthians 3:1-3 states, "Brothers, I could not address you as spiritual but as worldly—mere infants in Christ. I gave you milk, not solid food, for you were not yet ready for it. Indeed, you are still not ready. You are still worldly. For since there is jealousy and quarreling among you, are you not worldly? Are you not acting like mere men?" Thomas Moore says, "To be spiritual means to mature to a point beyond limited self-interest and anxiety about self."[54]

The writer of Hebrews says, "We have much to say about this, but it is hard to explain because you are slow to learn. In fact, though by this time you ought to be teachers, you need someone to teach you

---

[54] Thomas Moore, "Will We Take Moral Values Challenge?" *Spirituality & Health*, January/February 2005, 10-11.

the elementary truths of God's word all over again. You need milk, not solid foods! Anyone who lives on milk, being still an infant, is not acquainted with the teaching of righteousness. But solid food is for the mature, who by constant use have trained themselves to distinguish good from evil" (Heb. 5:11-14).

Spiritual Growth

Jesus grew by obedience and not only by study of the Torah. John 7:15-17 says, "The Jews were amazed and asked, 'How did this man get such learning without having studied?' Jesus answered, 'My teaching is not my own. It comes from him who sent me. If anyone chooses to do God's will, he will find whether my teaching comes from God or whether I speak on my own.'"

Luke wrote, "Then he went down to Nazareth with them and was obedient to them. But his mother treasured all these things in her heart. And Jesus grew in wisdom and stature, and in favor with God and men" (Luke 2:51-52). Jesus' obedience to His parents and His divine mission caused Him to experience growth and favor. As the writer of Hebrews said, "Although he was a son, he learned obedience from what he suffered and, once made perfect, he became the source of eternal salvation for all who obey him" (Heb. 5:8-9).

Devil's Tool

Disobedience leads to bondage, values drift and immaturity. Values drift is the slow erosion of our core values over time—those tiny changes can steer us off God's course. Jeremiah 7:23-24 described these values drift, "But I gave them this commandment: Obey me, and I will be your God and you will be my people. Walk in all the ways I command you, that it may go well with you. But they did not listen or pay attention; instead, they followed the stubborn inclination of their hearts. They went backward and not forward." Disobedience hinders our spiritual growth by making us slaves to sin, unable to hear and obey God. Jesus said, "I tell you the truth, everyone who sins is a slave to sin" (John 8:34).

The devil uses the tool of disobedience to enslave the disobedient to their sins. 2 Timothy 2:26 states, "And that they will come to their senses and escape the trap of the devil, who has taken them captive to do his will." The only power able to release us from sin and the devil's grip is the Truth, Jesus Christ (John 8:32). Samson's disobedience with Delilah demonstrated the destructive power of sin—it blinded him, enslaved and ultimately killed him (Judges 16:21, 16:30).

The devil leads us astray by corrupt company. King David said, "Blessed is the man who does not walk in the counsel of the wicked or stand in the way of sinners or sit in the seat of mockers" (Psalm 1:1). This verse describes the progression of sin as three verbs: walk, stand, and sit. We begin to walk or "hang out" with people of corrupt morals, allow them to have an impact on our behavior and tarnish our witness. Next, after a season of walking with them, we now stand with those sinners and begin to become desensitized to their evil deeds. Finally, after growing tired from standing and the social pressure to conform, we sit and join in their disobedience. Believers don't fall into sin; they walk away from innocence, step by step.

This vicious demonic cycle of regression is demonstrated by Abraham's nephew Lot. He set his heart on the fertile fields near Sodom. Genesis 13:11-13 says, "So Lot chose for himself the whole plain of the Jordan and set out toward the east. The two men parted company. Abraham lived in the land of Canaan, while Lot lived among the cities of the plain and pitched his tent near Sodom. Now the men of Sodom were wicked and were sinning greatly against the Lord."

Lot pitched his tent near Sodom (walk) in chapter thirteen of Genesis and by chapter nineteen he was living among the wicked people (stand). At the conclusion of chapter nineteen Lot conformed to the Sodomites' lifestyle (sit), as he was inebriated and had incestuous relationships with both of his daughters. The result of Lot's disobedience was the forming of two nations by his offspring, the Moabites and Ammonites; both of them were hostile enemies of Israel. Lot hung around junkyard dogs and got fleas!

The Process of Change

Psychologist James O. Prochaska's Transtheoretical Model of Behavior Change, "TTM," has five stages to achieve permanent behavioral change: precontemplation, contemplation, preparation, action, and maintenance. In the **precontemplation** stage the individual is unaware of their need for change or in denial. They may blame others or situational factors for their unhealthy behaviors or addictions. A simple definition of addiction is anything you cannot stop.

Precontemplators typically underestimate the pros of changing, overestimate the cons, and often are not aware of making such mistakes. The devil has blinded them from the truth and the destructive force of their sinful behavior. Dietrich Bonhoeffer describes this mindset in his statement, "As long as I am by myself in the confession of my sins everything remains in the dark but in the presence of a brother or sister the sin has to be brought into the light." In this stage believers and friends should encourage the individual to examine the effect of their behavior on others, their environment, and their own personal life as well as the benefits of change. This brings their darkness into the light of the truth.

In the **second** stage **contemplation**, the individual begins to realize they have a problem and need help. They realize some of the negative effects their unhealthy behavior has caused in their own life and their loved ones. The individual's blinders to the truth begin to fade and they examine the type of person they can become apart from that destructive behavior. In this stage believers should help them to come out of the darkness and into the light by being a model of Christ's love. St. Augustine said, "The confession of evil works is the first beginning of good works."

In the **third** stage, **preparation**, the individual has chosen to begin the process to take action to change within the next thirty days.

They take small steps they believe can help them make the healthy behavior a part of their daily lives. For example, they tell their friends and family they want to change their behavior. Friends and believers should give them love, continual support, and affirmation.

The **fourth** stage is **action**. The individual has now changed their unhealthy behavior within the past six months and is moving ahead on their road to recovery and freedom. They need to discover the power of conquering their urges and impulses through faith and commitment. In this stage accountability is huge; they need someone they can share their struggles with and not feel judged.

The **final** stage is **maintenance**. The person has changed their destructive behavior for more than six months and they are focused on continuing to move forward. It is important for people in this stage to be aware of situations that may tempt them to slip back into the unhealthy behavior—particularly stressful situations or places and people influencing them to perform the destructive behavior. Believers and friends should continue to pray for them and encourage them to be involved in a small group focused on their issues and offer them personal accountability.

Appetite

John Wesley said, "What we feed in our lives will grow." John Bevere said, "We will hunger for what we feed on." Jesus said, "Blessed are those who hunger and thirst for righteousness, for they will be filled." If we desire to grow spiritually we need to feed on the righteousness of God and put to death the desires of the flesh. King David said, "Let not my heart be drawn to what is evil, to take part in wicked deeds with men who are evildoers; let me not eat of their delicacies" (Psalm 141:4). As our flesh is put to death by obedience it loses its grip. A dead man or woman can never be tempted. Matthew Henry wrote, "The joy of the Lord will arm us against the assaults of our spiritual enemies and put our mouths out of taste for those pleasures with which the tempter baits his hooks."

When we feed the desires of the flesh our hearts will cease to hunger for God's presence because we are already filled. Suppose you eat an enormous Thanksgiving meal at lunch with turkey, stuffing, and mom's mashed potatoes, then at dinner you are offered a tastier meal of your favorite steak; you will cease to have a hunger for it because your cravings have already been satisfied. In the same way, if we feed on worldly pleasures we will not have an intense hunger and passion for God. Proverbs 27:7 states, "He who is full loathes honey, but to the hungry even what is bitter tastes sweet."

Our hunger for God is a spiritual thermometer that indicates our spiritual health. The first sign we are sick is our lack of appetite for food; so an absence of the desire to please God is a warning of spiritual sickness. A wrong diet of pleasures hinders our growth and leads to confusion of mind. Lot, unlike his Uncle Abraham, was unaware of God's soon coming wrath on Sodom (Gen 18:17). When we feed the flesh rather than live by the Spirit, we are like the bobcat who ate a porcupine and was in horrendous pain, unable to perceive the hunter in the bush.

Fruitful labor in the kingdom requires us to feed on the things of God. King Solomon said, "The laborer's appetite works for him; his hunger drives him on" (Prov. 16:26). As we hunger for God and His kingdom we will grow into maturity in Christ. King David said, "For God satisfies the thirsty and fills the hungry with good things." 1 Peter 2:2-3 says, "Like newborn babies, crave pure spiritual milk, so that by it you may grow up in your salvation, now that you have tasted that the Lord is good."

Growth & Loci of Control

In the tripolarity theory God and the individual's behavior bring spiritual growth and transformation. Paul wrote, "I planted the seed, Apollos watered it (internal locus), but God made it grow. So neither he who plants nor he who waters is anything, but only God, who makes things grow (external locus). The man who plants and the man who waters have one purpose and each will be rewarded according to his own labor" (1 Co. 3:6-8).

Hindrance of Growth

1 Peter 5:8 states, "Be self-controlled and alert. Your enemy the devil prowls around like a roaring lion looking for someone to devour." The devil hinders our spiritual growth by leading us astray from God and fellowship with His people. The African lion prowls for the elder male water buffalo that wanders from his herd. The elder water buffalo, from years of bunting and jostling with the younger bulls at the waterhole, begins to distance himself from the herd. Offended and wounded from the constant jostling, he slowly enters the bush. At first one king of the jungle prowls in the deep grass, than another, until finally the bull is surrounded and is helpless to defend himself.

The devil uses this same battle strategy to prevent spiritual maturity. A believer is offended and wounded by a fellow brother in Christ and quits attending his church and begins to associate with people who lack godly character. This leads him to drinking, drugs, or other vices before he realizes it his life is a whirlwind of confusion. Followers of Christ, in numbers, have great strength like snowflakes. Pastor Rick Warren said, "Christians, like snowflakes, are frail and weak, but when they stick together they can stop traffic."

Choice & Motivation

For growth to occur, we need to choose to follow Christ in obedience with humility. The motivation for transformation comes from having a hunger for God and the truth. Our hunger increases as we seek first the kingdom of God and set our hearts on following Christ. The source of strength to grow is the power of the Holy Spirit. As we put to death the flesh, the Spirit causes growth to occur; we are transformed from glory to glory into the image of Christ.

Summary

The tripolarity theory creates growth and transformation by our taking responsibility for our actions. We cannot blame our behavior only on external locus of control: "The devil made me do it! Or I guess that was just God's lot for my life and this is how I will always be!" There is both external and internal locus of control affecting our behavior and actions. St. Augustine taught in *City of God*, an individual's actions and behavior are a direct result of their heart's condition (good or evil) and the choices they make reflect their heart's true condition as it relates to God. Growth is allowing the good things God has sown in our hearts to harvest and weeding out the evil from the devil.

Chapter 9
Creation

In the beginning God created the heavens and the earth.

Genesis 1:1

By the word of the Lord were the heavens made,
their starry host by the breath of his mouth.

Psalms 33:6

There is no creature, regardless of its apparent insignificance that fails to display something of God's goodness and glory.

T. A. Kempis

Why is there something rather than nothing?

Lucian the Greek Skeptic 120-180 A.D.

Introduction

THE TRIPOLARITY THEORY in relationship to creation demonstrates that God has entrusted humanity with the responsibility of freedom of choice. As author Sir Laurens van der Post observed, "The greatest freedom conferred on us by God and human consciousness: the freedom to choose between good and evil; and as we choose, so shall we increase or decline."[55]

---

[55] Laurens van der Post, *A Walk with a White Bushman* (London: Chatto & Windus, 1986), 45-46.

The Father's creation was good and His grace permeated the earth. King David sang, "When you send your Spirit, they are created, and you renew the face of the earth" (Psalm 104:30). Origen in the second century stated, "The proximate goodness of any creature is best grasped in relation to the incomparable goodness of the triune God."

God's Goodness

Job 12:7-10 says, "Ask the animals, and they will teach you, or the birds of the air, and they will tell you; or speak to the earth, and it will teach you, or let the fish of the sea inform you. Which of all these does not know that the hand of the Lord has done this? In his hand is the life of every creature and the breath of all mankind." As I typed these powerful words, I peered out my front window to see a young sharp-shinned hawk attempting to take flight with an invasive vole. The eyesight of a hawk is incredible, being eight times more powerful than an average human's. If this hawk could read, it would be able to read a newspaper from seven stories high, or in this case see the vole in a field a mile away.

The majestic eyesight of the hawk testifies to God's perfect vision as Hebrews 4:13 describes, "Nothing in all creation is hidden from God's sight. Everything is uncovered and laid bare before the eyes of him to whom we must give account." The Father with His perfect sight sees and blesses His children.

I joyfully watched two coyotes playfully chase each other in a vacant field a mile from my home. These were Selah moments that gave me a glimpse of God's glory in creation. Karl Barth said, "Humanity is never dismissed from the wonder that forms the root of sound theology." Elizabeth Barrett Browning observed, "Earth's crammed with heaven, and every common bush afire with God; but only he who sees takes off his shoes. The rest sit around it and pluck blackberries."

Approximately two weeks after I experienced the coyotes' joyful playing, while I was eating breakfast at six in the morning, I witnessed a spotted fawn frantically scurrying into the brush from a deadly predator. Hot on her trail was a coyote ready for a Bambi dinner.[56] These two events demonstrate both the wonder of creation and the upheaval and violence.[57] Philip Yancey said, "Everything that we humans touch gives off both the original scent of goodness and the foul odor of fallenness, and requires the slow work of redemption."

William Robinson describes this wonder and terror,

> "Nature always has a double aspect. It presents itself as benign, ready to do more than cooperate with man's endeavor to reach happiness. And it presents itself as hostile, destroying in a single night all that man has built up through long years of research and toil, sometimes appearing to take on even a malignant aspect, as if mocked and derided the high endeavor of man's spirit."[58]

Even the violence in the animal kingdom from the fall will be restored at Christ's return. Isaiah 65:25 says, "The wolf and the lamb will feed together, and the lion will eat straw like the ox, but dust will be the serpent's food. They will neither harm nor destroy on all my holy mountains, says the Lord."

On a more humorous note the wonder and terror in creation can be seen by people's unique experiences with squirrels. My Aunt Jennie had a squirrel, Chatter, who knocked (scratched) at her door

---

[56] Now imagine your perspective of seeing a coyote in your yard if one killed your beloved pet. In our present age, nature exhibits both wonder and terror and this can create both praise and despair.

[57] In the Garden of Eden animals were herbivores and only after the flood were there carnivores (Genesis 9).

[58] William Robinson, *The Devil and God* (Nashville: Abingdon-Cokesbury, 1945), 16.

and she hand-fed peanuts. As a child, watching this friendly squirrel brought delight. My supervisor Dwayne Clark had a terror experience with a furry free-falling squirrel. After Dwayne shaved his head, he went for a midsummer walk near his home and a squirrel fell from the top of hundred foot oak tree just barely missing his head. Dwayne joked, "If I had any hair it would have stood straight up as I saw the kamikaze coming right at my unprotected head!"

Professor Carol Harrison wrote,

> "In our fallen condition, even profitable labor is distasteful to us. We are beset by numerous threats to our physical and spiritual health, so that exile, disease, sudden death, demonic attacks, and famine are not uncommon. At the same time, St. Augustine in his writings contemplates the extraordinary blessing that God gives humans, including existence, fitting bodies (hands, erect posture, voice, internal organs, and so forth), procreation, rationality, the arts, agricultural and technological development, poetry and philosophy, and above all the ability to attain eternal life by grace. The beauty and diversity of the natural creation likewise manifest God's bounty."[59]

Nature & the Bible

One of my favorite animal videos is from the movie *The Meerkat* (2008).[60] In this film, a young twelve-week-old meerkat, Kolo, is pursued by a martial eagle. Kolo desperately escapes down his burrow, only to discover a cape cobra waiting in the dark. He instantly turned a corner with the cobra on his heels, rushed out of his home, back into the Kalahari Desert sun. Just as the six-foot coil

---

[59] Carol Harrison, *Beauty and Revelation in the Thought of Saint Augustine* (Oxford: Clarendon, 1992) 131-33, 160-62.

[60] *The Meerkat*, Weinstein Company and BBC Films (2008).

of muscle reared to strike Kolo from behind, the eagle swooped down and with her talons, flew off with a cobra sandwich.

St. Augustine said, "God's two books are nature and the Bible. Let the Bible be a book for you so that you may hear God's voice, let the sphere of the world be a book for you so that you might see the Creator in action."

Divine Virtues

The animal kingdom reveals divine virtues. The African honey badger, crowned the most fearless animal in the world, has the attributes of chutzpah. This thirty-pound creature, with leather-tough skin and razor-sharp claws and teeth, refuses to back down to any challenger. The honey badger will boldly attack and defeat even the most furious beast in the savanna such as a ten-foot-long monitor, leopards, cheetahs (biting them below the belt), venomous puff adders, and jackals. In an *Animal Planet* video, a courageous, hungry honey badger preyed upon a cape cobra.[61] The nine-foot-long reptile frantically struck the badger repeatedly as it continued to tear into its tender head.

The badger, non-immune to the cobra's venom, collapsed; a few hours later awoke from his somnolent hangover and finished his delicacy.[62] A honey badger will travel over forty kilometers a day for food and break into honeybee hives to feast on larva. This chutzpah modeled by the honey badger is the same boldness and faith God desires from His children. True faith is steadfast trust in the goodness of God. Professor Brad Young said, "When Jesus praises people for faith, often they have demonstrated extreme persistence in attempting to reach him for help. This unwavering perseverance combined with a bold belief in God is often related to the essence of the word "faith" in the Gospels."[63]

---

[61] AnimalPlanet.com: Most Fearless Animal—Honey Badger

[62] One bite of a cape cobra is venomous enough to kill six humans.

[63] Brad H. Young, *The Parables* (Massachusetts: Hendrickson, 1998), 55.

Types of Revelation

Theologians teach two types of revelation revealing God's presence in creation: general and special. These two types of revelation are referred as the small lowercase "t" truth for general revelation and big uppercase "T" Truth for special revelation. General revelation consists of revelation that is given to all humanity such as nature and creation. An example of general revelation is the earth's average distance from the sun is ninety-three million miles. If the earth was closer to the sun, by even a few miles, the temperature of the earth would be too high to sustain life; if further away, our planet would be a frozen sphere. St. Thomas Aquinas's *Summa Theologica* is based on natural revelation, since he used five philosophical arguments to prove God's existence.

Romans 1:20 describes natural revelation, "For since the creation of the world God's invisible qualities—his eternal power and divine nature—have been clearly seen, being understood from what has been made, so that men are without excuse."

Natural revelation demonstrates the creative wonder of God, but only through special revelation can a person have a relationship with their Creator. Loraine Boettner said, "Fallen humanity is comparable to a bird with a broken wing. This bird is 'free' to fly, but is unable to do so. Likewise, 'the natural man' is free to come to God, but unable. How can he repent of his sin when he loves it? How can he come to God when he is at enmity with Him?"[64]

Special Revelation

Special revelation is given directly from God: the Bible, Holy Spirit, prophecy, salvation history, resurrection, Trinity, and the incarnation. Millard J. Erickson said, "Because humankind is finite and God is infinite, we cannot know or fellowship with Him unless

---

[64] Loraine Boettner, *The Reformed Doctrine of Predestination*, 8th ed. (Grand Rapids: Eerdmans, 1958), 62.

He reveals Himself to us."[65] Professor Cornelius Van Til wrote, "The revelation of a self-sufficient God can have no meaning for a mind that thinks of itself as ultimately autonomous."[66]

The Apostle Peter's great confession is an example of special revelation. Matthew 16:15-17 says, "But what about you?" Jesus asked. "Who do you say I am?" Simon Peter answered, "You are the Christ, the Son of the living God." Jesus replied, "Blessed are you, Simon son of Jonah, for this was not revealed to you by man, but by my Father in heaven."

Peter's confession of the Christ demonstrates the tripolarity theory. God revealed Jesus' identity to Peter, and he chose to believe the truth, and the devil attempted to deceive Peter away from the truth. After Peter gave the confession, Jesus redefined the meaning of Messiah, as the suffering servant (Matt. 16:21). Peter experienced a Copernican paradigm shift and exclaimed, "Never Lord! This shall never happen to you!" (Matt. 16:22). Jesus, in response to Peter's diametrically opposed statement, said, "Get behind me, Satan! You are a stumbling block to me; you do not have in mind the things of God, but the things of men" (Matt. 16:23).

Peter, in response to God's special revelation, decided to follow Jesus, even unto martyrdom. John 6:67-68 states, "You do not want to leave too, do you?" Jesus asked the Twelve. Simon Peter answered him, "Lord, to whom shall we go? You have the words of eternal life."

Trinity

The tripolarity theory demonstrates the tripartite God created the universe from nothing (*ex nihilo*). Isaiah 44:24 states, "This is what the Lord says—your Redeemer, who formed you in the womb: I am

---

[65] Millard J. Erickson, *Introducing Christian Doctrine* (Grand Rapids: Baker Books, 1992), 34.

[66] Cornelius Van Til, *Christian Apologetics* (Phillipsburg: Presbyterian and Reformed Pub., 1976), 54.

the Lord, who has made all things, who alone stretch out the heavens, who spread out the earth by myself." This verse clearly states that God created the universe by Himself. If God created the earth by Himself and Jesus and the Holy Spirit were involved in creation then they are also God.

The Scriptures teach that the Father, Jesus, and the Holy Spirit (the Trinity) created the world. John wrote testifying about Jesus, "Through him all things were made; without him nothing was made that has been made" (John 1:3). The Apostle Paul states the Father was the Creator in Romans 11:36: "For from him and through him and to him are all things." Genesis 1:2 and Psalms 104:30 implement the Holy Spirit's role in creation as, "Bringing light out of the darkness and order from chaos." St. Athanasius of Alexandra said, "If your Savior is not your Creator then you are not saved."

Presuppositions

Only by faith can an individual believe God created the world and this faith requires special revelation from the Holy Spirit. Christian Apologists in the second century had the proposition Latin statement *impossibile est sine deo discere deum*—it is impossible to learn to know God without the help of God. St. Augustine said, "I wished to be made just as certain of things that I could not see, as I was certain that seven and three make ten."

Peter wrote about creation and said, "But they deliberately forget that long ago by God's word the heavens existed and the earth was formed out of water and by water. By these waters also the world of that time was deluged and destroyed" (2 Peter 3:5-6). In these verses, Peter describes the days right before the eschaton, and the scoffers who mocked divine creation and Christ's return. They denied these doctrines based on their desires to live for pleasures and not repent of their sins (2 Peter 3:3, Jude 16).

True faith is a commitment to follow God from the head to the feet. In our heads we believe in God (knowledge), with the heart we have a desire to love Him (will), and with our feet we respond in service.

Atheists' Presuppositions

The presupposition of atheism, as with theism, requires faith.[67] Disproving the existence of God is beyond the scope of science, and would require both omniscience and omnipresence, and thus make the atheist a god. John Polkinghorne states, "Science investigates a physical world that is open to the manipulative investigation of our experimental enquiry. Theology seeks to speak of the God who is to be encountered in awe and obedience, and who is not available to be subjected to our testing interrogation."[68]

The U.S. National Academy of Sciences in 1985 issued a valid explanation of the relationship between science and religion:

> "At the root of the apparent conflict between some religions and evolution is a misunderstanding of the critical difference between religious and scientific ways of knowing. Religions and science answer different questions about the world. Whether there is a purpose to the universe for human existence are not questions for science. Religious and scientific ways of knowing have played, and will continue to play, significant roles in human history."[69]

Our presuppositions determine our beliefs. German Enlightenment Philosopher Gotthold Ephraim Lessing said,

> "The accidental truths of history can never become the proof of necessary truths of reason . . . This, then, 'is the ugly broad ditch which I cannot get across,

---

[67] See endnotes: Historical definition of atheism and contemporary meaning.

[68] John Polkinghorne, *Belief in God in an Age of Science* (New Haven: Yale University Press, 1998), 37.

[69] *Teaching about Evolution and the Nature of Science* (Washington, D.C.: National Academy of Sciences Press, 1998), 58.

however often and however earnestly I have tried to make the leap. Since the truth of these miracles has completely ceased to be demonstrable by miracles still happening now, since they are no more than historical reports of miracles, I deny that they should bind me in the least to a faith in the other teaching of Christ.'"[70]

British Enlightenment Philosopher Bernard Russell, an atheist, stated, "If I stand before the judgment seat of God, I'll look God straight in the eye and say, 'There just was not enough evidence for me to believe!'" Russell also wrote in his defense of atheism,

"That man is the product of causes which had no prevision of the end they were achieving; that his origin, his growth, his hopes and fears, his loves and beliefs are but the outcome of accidental collocations of atoms; that no fire, no heroism, no intensity of thought and feeling, can preserve an individual life beyond the grave; that all the labors of the age, all the devotion, all the inspiration, all the noonday brightness of human genius are destined to extinction."[71]

Atheist Astronomer Carl Sagan's presupposition was, "The cosmos is all that is or ever was or ever will be." In December 1996, a few weeks before his death, he was interviewed by Ted Koppel on *Nightline*. He was at the threshold of death and Koppel asked him, "Dr. Sagan, do you have any pearls of wisdom that you like to impart to the human race?" Sagan replied:

"We live on a hunk of rock and metal that circles a humdrum star that is one of 400 billion other stars that

---

[70] Gotthold Ephraim Lessing, *Lessing's Theological Writings*, translated by Henry Chadwick (Stanford University Press, 1957), 51-55.

[71] Bertrand Russell, *Why I Am Not a Christian* (New York: Simon & Schuster, 1957), 107.

make up the Milky Way Galaxy, which is one of billions of other galaxies, which make up a universe, which may be one of a very large number—perhaps an infinite number—of other universes. That is a perspective on human life and our culture that is well worth pondering."[72]

Robert Green Ingersoll (1833-1899), nicknamed The Great Agnostic, described the bleak scenario of a universe without God at the graveside funeral of his beloved atheist brother who had died suddenly. In his funeral message, Robert Ingersoll preached the horror of his own presupposition there is no Creator:

> "Whether in mid-sea or among breakers of the farther shore, a wreck must mark at last the end of each and all. And every life, no matter if its every hour is rich with love and every moment jeweled with joy, will, at its close, become a tragedy, as sad, and deep, and dark as can be woven of the warp and woof of mystery and death . . . Life is a narrow vale between the cold and barren peaks of two eternities. We strive in vain to look beyond the heights. We cry aloud, and the only answer is the echo of our wailing cry."

Our presuppositions determine our interpretation of the epistemology of creation. Is humanity created in the image of God as the theorists believe or were we created by time and chance? The theorist belief offers hope of an afterlife while the atheist presupposition inevitably leads to a sense of despair. As Carl Wallace Miller observed, "Belief of God is acceptance of the basic principle that the universe makes sense, that there is behind it an ultimate purpose."

---

[72] Carl Sagan, *ABC News Nightline*, December 4, 1996.

Astronomer Robert Jastrow wrote concerning the discovery that our universe had a beginning,

> "For the scientist who has lived by his faith and presupposition in the power of reason alone, the story ends like a bad dream. He has scaled the mountains of ignorance; he is about to conquer the highest peak; as he pulls himself over the final rock, he is greeted by a band of theologians who have been sitting there for centuries."[73]

Theodicy

If God's creation was good and holy, as the Bible testifies, then what is the causation of evil?[74] Theodicy is the defense of God's goodness and omnipotence in relationship with the existence of evil. Jeffrey Burton Russell wrote, "The most poignant aspect of the problem of evil for Judaism, Christianity, Islam, and all monotheist religions is the reconciliation of God's power and goodness with the existence of evil."[75]

Every religion since the dawn of civilization has attempted to answer this enigma. One sect of Gnosticism in the first century taught, "That there had to be a hierarchy of demiurge mini gods in the process of creation because an all-powerful and benevolent Creator would not create an imperfect universe." Bart D. Ehrman wrote, "Most Gnostics assumed that evil is written into the fabric of the material world itself."[76] These Gnostics failed to realize evil was a result of humanity's freedom of choice, which allowed the fall to occur, and the creation was originally good (Gen. 1:31).

---

[73] Robert Jastrow, *God and the Astronomers*, second ed. (New York: W.W. Norton & Company, 1992), 105.

[74] See endnotes: Three main traditional views of evil.

[75] Jeffrey Burton Russell, *Lucifer: The Devil in the Middle Ages* (Ithaca and London: Cornell University Press, 1984), 307.

[76] Bart D. Ehrman, *Lost Christianities* (New York: Oxford Press, 2003), 116.

The Gnostics' analysis of creation is equivalent to hoodlums spray-painting the Mona Lisa and hundreds of years later an art critic examining the damaged masterpiece and screaming, "Leonardo da Vinci never would have painted this piece of art because it is flawed."

Christian and Jewish philosophers explain evil in creation by the statement, "When God creates, He makes something less than Himself and this leaves room for imperfection because the created is always less than the Creator." This statement is an adequate explanation for the problem of evil, but it does not give a comprehensive answer that will end all doubt and lead to faith. Since skepticism is born in the heart and presuppositions of the beholder — the battle of faith is fought more in the heart than in the mind.

Dr. Ronald Meyers said, "God best demonstrates His glory using faulty tools." Imagine for a moment seeing a huge million-dollar mansion with hundreds of rooms and a deluxe swimming pool. Then the contractor shows you a broken hammer, a bent screwdriver, and a beaten-down Caterpillar construction vehicle, and says, "These were the only tools we used to build this magnificent mansion!" Our gut reaction would be skepticism and we would think they are playing a joke.

God, through His creation, reconciles weak and sinful proclivity in humanity, and transforms their darkness into His light. In redemption, God uses ordinary and obedient people to fulfill His purpose. 2 Corinthians 4:7 says, "But we have this treasure in jars of clay to show that this all-surpassing power is from God and not from us.'"

Free Will

The Book of Wisdom in the LXX translation and listed among the classifications deuterocanonical and Apocrypha states, "For God created the human to be immortal, He made him as an image of His own nature; death came into the cosmos only through the Devil's envy, as those who belong to him find to their cost" (Wisdom 2:23-24). Genesis 1:27 says, "So God created man in his own image, in the image of God he created him; male and female he created them." God created humanity not as a mechanical submissive robot, but with the freedom of will, so their love would be pure.

The limit of external locus of control (God) in the tripolarity theory with relationship to free choice is demonstrated with the creation narrative. The biblical writer states: God said, "Let there be light," and it was so; God said, "Let the land be separated from the water," and it was so; God, said, "Let there be creatures on land," and it was so. Once the creation was complete, God commanded Adam not to eat from the tree of knowledge of good and evil, but the text does not say, like the rest of the creation narrative, "it was so," because humanity, unlike nature, was given free will.

The Devil

The devil, the crafty serpent in the Garden of Eden, had a free will and his pride led to his fall. Job 26:13 states, "By his Spirit he hath garnished the heavens; his hand hath formed the crooked serpent." The devil was formed by God as a beautiful majestic angelic being and for the purpose of worshipping the Creator. Ezekiel 28:12 states, "You were the model of perfection, full of wisdom and perfect in beauty." The devil's pride in his attributes caused him to rebel. This cosmic rebellion resulted in the creation to be in upheaval.

Redemption

Poet James Joyce said, "History is a nightmare from which I am trying to awake." The fall caused the dream paradise Eden to be deluged into the nightmare we call planet earth. In the tripolarity theory, God is the primary agent in redemption transforming evil for His glory. Ephesians 2:10 states, "For we are God's work of art created in Christ Jesus for good works which God prepared beforehand in order that we might walk in them."[77]

ORU had a campus student fun day. During their event, an artist created scratch board art. This scratch board art was formed by spraying five layers of different colors of spray paint and then carving out of the darkness a masterful panoply painting. This artist made me a scratch board art plaque of a futurist city with bluish-green waterfalls and a red moon. In redemption, like the scratch board art, Christ cuts through our layers of failures, sins, and pain (the blackness) and transforms them for His glory.

I was reminded in my first year of seminary of Christ's redemptive power, when I discovered, in my parents' basement, an envelope with files on my learning disabilities due to autism. The files contained reports written by renowned neurological psychologist Dr. Jerel E. Del Dotto and he stated in his report, "Due to Ron's severe learning disability, he may never read beyond the seventh-grade comprehension level or be able to attend college." By God's grace (external locus) and my hard work (internal locus) these predictions were not fulfilled. Christ reconciled my learning disability and enabled me to graduate with a 3.9 G.P.A., Summa Cum Laude, and earn a Master of Divinity with a perfect 4.0 G.P.A. and highest honors. We serve in Christ's redemption as living testimony to God's glory.

Christ's death and resurrection has restored the effects of the fall and brought redemption for the community of believers. In the gospel of John, Christ's death and resurrection inaugurates a new creation restoring humanity's relationship with the Father. Genesis 2:7 states, "The Lord God formed the man from the dust of the ground and breathed into his nostrils the breath of life, and the man became a living being."

---

[77] Ron Sandison's translation from the Greek.

When Christ appeared to the eleven disciples after His resurrection, John records, "And with that Jesus breathed on them and said, "Receive the Holy Spirit'" (John 20:22). This redemptive act demonstrates that the disciples now have been born again by the power of the Holy Spirit (John 3).

As the source of life Jesus has redeemed us. In Genesis 3:3, Eve tells the serpent that God told them that they must not eat or touch the tree of knowledge of good and evil. After Jesus' resurrection in John's Gospel, Christ tells Mary Magdalene in the garden, "Do not touch me" (John 20:17). The linguistic link between John 20:17 and Genesis 3:3 is exact; both state in Greek, μη αψησθε αυτου, "Don't touch." Mary Magdalene's encounter with the risen Christ demonstrates redemption has come—its full effects will only be revealed at Christ's return.

Summary

The glory of God's creation empowers us to preach the good news to all creation and participate in Christ's redemption. The Apostle Paul said, "We are therefore Christ's ambassadors, as though God were making his appeal through us. We implore you on Christ's behalf: Be reconciled to God" (2 Cor. 5:20).

Chapter 10
The Fall

Any discussion of how suffering fits into God's scheme ultimately leads back to the cross.

Philip Yancey

The Christian has a great advantage over other men, not by being less fallen than they, nor less doomed to live in a fallen world, but by knowing that he is a fallen man in a fallen world.

C.S Lewis

He has made everything beautiful in its time. He has also set eternity in the hearts of men; yet they cannot fathom what God has done from beginning to end.

Ecclesiastes 3:11

For our light and momentary troubles are achieving for us an eternal glory that far outweighs them all. So we fix our eyes not on what is seen, but on what is unseen. For what is seen is temporary, but what is unseen is eternal.

2 Corinthians 4:17-18

Introduction

SEPTEMBER 11, 2001, my roommate shouted, "You need to see this; an airplane just hit the World Trade Center!" One quote that has stuck with me all these years was a CNN journalist's statement, "A survivalist is not someone who is smarter, stronger, or more educated, but someone who understands the seriousness of the present time and acts accordingly."

A year later, I participated with my ORU buddy Dave Harden in the *American Heroes'* celebration for the families of 9/11 in Washington, D.C. I was reminded of this statement as I had a conversation with a father whose thirty-year-old son was a passenger on American Airlines Flight 77 which crashed into the Pentagon. This father proudly described his son, a Harvard medical school graduate, as exceptionally bright, athletic, six-foot-two in stature, and strong as an ox.

Then he said with a tear, "The thing that upsets me the most about his senseless death was he and the rest of the passengers did nothing to stop the terrorists because they did not understand the present crisis!"

Present Crisis

The Apostle Paul said, "And do this, understanding the present time. The hour has come for you to wake up from your slumber, because our salvation is nearer now than when we first believed. The night is nearly over; the day is almost here. So let us put aside the deeds of darkness and put on the armor of light" (Rom. 13:11-12). The present time in view of eternity causes believers to have an urgency to live with purpose, realizing that life is short—we are not promised tomorrow.

On September 11, 2001, the passengers on the two flights crashing into the World Trade Center and those on Flight 77 smashing into the Pentagon did not fully understand the horror unfolding. They did not know, as the CNN journalist stated, "How to respond in their hour of crisis."

The passengers on the delayed United Airlines Flight 93 crashing in a field in Pennsylvania had an advantage in knowing how to respond to the present crisis; they had already heard the reports about the other flights' demise and their heroic actions saved many lives.

Only Flight 93 did not reach the terrorists' intended target. Passenger Todd Beamer, a Wheaton graduate and Christian, used a credit card phone in the back of the plane to try and notify authorities of the terrorist hijackers' plot. Instead of contacting emergency personnel, the operator transferred him to GTE supervisor Lisa Jefferson, a fellow Christian. Todd informed Lisa of their crisis and they both recited the Lord's Prayer. Todd then gathered the other male passengers and his last audible words were, "Are you guys ready? Okay, let's roll!"

Lisa Beamer, the wife of Todd, wrote, "The words 'Let's roll!' were especially significant to me. Just hearing that made me smile, partially because it was 'so Todd,' but also because it showed my husband felt he could still do something positive in the midst of a crisis situation."[78] These words describe the response we should have in the present in view of eternity. The Apostle Paul said, "Be very careful, then, how you live—not as unwise but as wise, making the most of every opportunity, because the days are evil" (Eph. 5:15-16).

Paradise Lost

The tripolarity theory views the earth as fallen from her paradise condition in the Garden of Eden and digressed through the effects of sin to her present state. This source of digression was a result of both free choice and the natural processes of the universe tainted by the fall. Romans 8:19-22 states,

> "The creation waits in eager expectation for the sons of God to be revealed. For the creation was subjected to frustration, not by its own choice, but by the will of the one who subjected it, in hope that the creation itself will be liberated from its bondage to decay and brought into the glorious freedom of the children of God. We know that the whole creation has been

---

[78] Lisa Beamer with Ken Abraham, *Let's Roll!* (Grand Rapids: Zondervan, 2002), 187.

groaning in the pains of childbirth right up to the present time."

The first book in the Bible, Genesis, describes the degeneration of this once beautiful planet by the fall. Everything God created in the creation account was said to be good. Genesis 2:6 states, "But the streams came up from the earth and watered the whole surface of the ground." Before the fall there were no famines or floods.

There were also no nuisances of thorns and weeds in the garden. Genesis 3:18 states, "The ground will produce thorns and thistles for you, and you will eat the plants of the field." Weeds can harbor and spread pathogens—infectious germs or bacterial agents. One of the principle pathways whereby pathogens can invade a host is through soil contamination such as weeds. Soil contamination has the longest and most persistent potential for harboring a pathogen. Types of pathogens include viral, bacterial, fungal, prionic, and other parasites. Thus, prior to the fall and the curse of the ground by God, there were no diseases like the 1918 influenza virus or the Black Plague as the soil and water conditions were pure.

In the Garden of Eden, there were only perfect weather conditions, and no harmful aging effects due to the sun's radiation. The creation account states there was a canopy over the earth (Gen. 1:7-8, 2:5, 7:11). This canopy of water over the earth protected humanity from the sun's harmful rays and enabled them to have a lifespan in the hundreds of years. Genesis chapter five mentions humanity's longevity in its genealogy: Adam lived 930 years, Seth the son of Adam lived 912 years, and Methuselah lived 969 years. Thus before the fall there were no premature deaths.

Downward Spiral

The book of Genesis demonstrates a progression of degeneration upon humanity. In chapter three of Genesis, Adam and Eve disobeyed God and He proclaimed their punishment of death. In Genesis chapter four, death made his smashing appearance with Cain killing his brother Abel. In chapters six and seven, humanity's continuous rebellion resulted in God sending a universal flood. Genesis 6:5 says, "The Lord saw how great man's wickedness on the earth had become, and that every inclination of the thoughts of his heart was only evil all the time."

God brought a flood upon the earth by causing the canopy to break forth with rain for forty days and nights, but He protected Noah and his family (Gen. 7:24). Humanity after the antediluvian period ceased to have a lifespan in the hundreds of years. Chapter eleven in Genesis records the first seismic activity with the continental drift of the supercontinent Pangaea as God dispersed humanity over the whole earth for building the Tower of Babel.

Genesis 10:25 and 1 Chronicles 1:19 states, "Two sons were born to Eber: One was named Peleg, because in his time the earth was divided; his brother was named Joktan." The name Peleg in the LXX Greek translation is derived from two main Greek words, παντα meaning all and γη meaning land or earth. Thus Peleg was named in memory of the period of history before all the continents divided. It is interesting to note that only in 1915 with the publication of *The Origin of Continents and Oceans* by Alfred Wegener was this theory widely accepted, over 6,000 years after Peleg.

Prior to the Tower of Babel the whole world had one language and common speech (Gen. 11:1). A mighty warrior, Nimrod, united the people of the earth to build a tower reaching into the heavens. God, in response to their hubristic building program, confused their language and scattered the people over the earth. Genesis 11:9 states, "That is why it was called Babel—because there the Lord confused the language of the whole world. From there the Lord scattered them over the face of the whole earth."

God scattered the people of the earth by separating the supercontinent of Pangaea and creating movement in the seven tectonic plates. This movement of the tectonic plates, geologists have termed continental drift. Earthquakes and volcanic activity, mountain-building, and ocean trench formation now occur along these plate boundaries. Prior to the Tower of Babel and the fall there were no earthquakes or tsunamis.

It is ironic that in the English term "tectonic plate," "tectonic" is derived from the Greek word τεκτονικος meaning "pertaining to building." It was the building of the Tower of Babel and God's judgment which set these plates in motion. Jesus predicted earthquakes and other natural disasters would increase just before His return (Luke 21:11).

The book of Genesis explains the terrorist attacks of 9/11 and the conflict in the Middle East. Abraham was promised a son and through his offspring descendants as numerous as the stars in the sky and countless as the sand of the seashore (Gen. 12:1-3). In haste and with his wife Sarah's permission, Abraham attempted to fulfill God's promise by having a son with his wife's handmaiden. Genesis 16:11-12 records, "The angel of the Lord said to Hagar, 'You are now with child and you will have a son. You shall name him Ishmael, for the Lord has heard of your misery. He will be a wild donkey of a man; his hand will be against everyone and everyone's hand against him, and he will live in hostility toward all his brothers.'"

The angel of the Lord predicted Ishmael's descendants would be wild donkeys of men and at war against all the other nations. Until Christ's return there will continue to be unrest in the Middle East region due to the birth of Ishmael and our human nature. Jesus said, "They will fall by the sword and will be taken as prisoners to all nations. Jerusalem will be trampled on by the Gentiles until the times of the Gentiles are fulfilled" (Luke 21:24).

Genesis explains all our heartfelt questions, "the eternity in our hearts," and reveals the effects of the fall which has caused the earth's present hostile conditions. Theologian David Bentley Hart wrote, "To see the world in its fallen state is to rejoice and mourn at once, to regard the world as a mirror of infinite beauty, but as glimpsed through the veil of death; it is to see creation in chains, but beautiful as in the beginning of days."[79]

General & Specific

St. Theresa of Avila said, "From the perspective of heaven the most miserable life on earth will appear as one bad night in an inconvenient hotel." Jesus said, "I have told you these things, so that in me you may have peace. In this world you will have trouble. But take heart! I have overcome the world" (John 16:33). In this present life, the Bible promises us due to the fall, we will have hardships.

The general cause perspective is bad things happen in this fallen world—the best response is to grow through these circumstances with faith (external locus) and actions (internal locus). We will not always understand the reasons for our hardships but we can always respond with faith and obedience.

Focusing on the general cause encourages individuals not to try and figure out exactly "why or what" caused something to occur, i.e., was it God, the devil, natural processes, or human agents; but "how" they will respond. Dorothee Solle said, "When tragedy and suffering occurs we must not ask why or where did it come from, but where will it lead us and how can we grow from it."[80]

A general cause statement is: "There was a fall, and sin and death are a result of this fall, so my uncle's death of cancer is part of life in a fallen world." This statement acknowledges their uncle's death was outside one's locus of control and external. A specific cause statement is: "The devil caused the death of my uncle by cancer," "God needed another saint in His choir so He took him home," or "My uncle being around secondhand smoke at work caused the cancer."

---

[79] David Bentley Hart, *The Doors of the Sea: Where was God in the Tsunami?* (Grand Rapids: Eerdmans, 2005), 61.

[80] Dorothee Solle, *Thinking About God* (Texas: Trinity Press, 1987), 145.

Response

The theology of Jesus focused on the general cause leading to response and growth rather than the specific cause that can lead to guilt, fear, blame, or confusion. Luke writes,

> "Now there were some present at that time who told Jesus about the Galileans whose blood Pilate had mixed with their sacrifices. Jesus answered, 'Do you think that these Galileans were worse sinners than all the other Galileans because they suffered this? I tell you, no! But unless you repent, you too will all perish. Or those eighteen who died when the tower in Siloam fell on them—do you think they were more guilty than all the others living in Jerusalem? I tell you no but unless you repent, you too will all perish" (Luke 13:1-5).

This dialogue discussion was concerning loci of control; was the death of these Galileans internal locus or external? The internal locus of control (human choice) is the people made Pilate angry by their sacrifices so Pilate had them killed for their actions; the tower in Siloam was poorly designed so it fell, killing eighteen people who chose to enter it.

The external locus of control (fate, luck, or powerful other) is the Galileans died because they made God angry with their sacrifices, or the eighteen in the Tower of Siloam were in the wrong place at the wrong time (fate), or God waited until the exact right eighteen were in the tower and then He made it crash down (divine wrath).

Jesus does not focus on the loci of control (specific cause) like his audience, but the response (general cause), "Unless you repent, you too will all perish." He uses these events to challenge his audience to mature by turning, with faith in God and examining their own lives and actions.

The real issue is not "why or how" the crisis occurred, but the actions and choices the individual takes in response to it. Helen

Keller states, "Although the world is full of suffering, it is full also of the overcoming of it." The narrative of Job demonstrates this response of faith and obedience in crisis.

Book of Job

The book of Job never answers the question of suffering or the problem of good and evil, and it also does not explain the inconsistencies in Deuteronomistic theology, but instead teaches faithfulness to God in the midst of a fallen world. In Arabic, Job's name is a verb and means "to turn back or repent"; these are words of response and action. In Hebrew, "Job" is a passive verb and simply means "the hated one" or "the persecuted," describing his conditions of suffering.

This narrative begins stating that in the land of Uz there lived a man named Job, and this man was righteous, blameless, and God-fearing. Job was a family man who had seven sons and three daughters and he was the greatest man among all the people of the east (Job 1:3). The angels and Satan came one day to present themselves before God and God boasted to Satan, "Have you consider my servant Job? There is no one on earth like him; he is blameless and upright, a man who fears God and shuns evil!" (Job 1:8).

In response to God's praise, Satan attacked Job's character and challenged his motives. Job 1:9-12 states,

> "'Does Job fear God for nothing?' Satan replied. 'Have you not put a hedge around him and his household and everything he has? You have blessed the work of his hands, so that his flocks and herds are spread throughout the land. But stretch out your hand and strike everything he has, and he will surely curse you to your face.' The Lord said to Satan, 'Very well, then, everything he has is in your hands, but on the man himself do not lay a finger.' Then Satan went out from the presence of the Lord."

Tempter

Satan required God's permission to test Job so he could lay hold of Job, his possessions, and his family. Even the legions of demons had to receive permission from Jesus to enter the herd of pigs (Luke 8:32). Thus in the tripolarity theory, Satan's power, unlike God's, is limited. Satan devised a scheme to destroy Job's faith. First, Satan incited the Sabeans tribe to kill Job's servants and plunder his livestock. Satan caused fire to come down from heaven and devour his sheep and some of his servants. The devil's final onslaught on Job's possessions was three Chaldeans' raids, killing the rest of his servants and stealing his camels.

Next, Satan brought destruction on Job's home by sending a desert wind killing his seven sons and three daughters (Job 1:17). The only family member that Satan allowed to live was Job's nagging wife, whose famous line in the narrative is "Curse God and die!" (Job 2:9-10).

Job's Response

Job responded to his tragic loss by tearing his robe, shaving his head, and worshipping God, saying, "Naked I came from my mother's womb, and naked I will depart. The Lord gave and the Lord has taken away; may the name of the Lord be praised" (Job 1:21). The biblical writer asserts the statement, "In all this, Job did not sin by charging God with wrongdoing" (Job 1:22). Job remained steadfast to God and praised Him in the midst of his loss. The source of Job's obedience was not the hedge of protection or his great riches as Satan had claimed, but his love for his Creator.

Round Two

Satan refused defeat and approached God again and said, "Skin for skin! A man will give all he has for his own life. But stretch your hand and strike his flesh and bones, and he will surely curse you to your face" (Job 2:4-5). Once more God gave Satan permission to wreak havoc on Job's life; the only restriction this round was that Satan could not physically kill him. Job 1:7 says, "So Satan went out from the presence of the Lord and afflicted Job with painful sores from the soles of his feet to the top of his head." Job, in unbearable pain, sat in ashes and with a piece of broken pottery scraped his sores. The biblical writer again reiterates, "In all this, Job did not sin in what he said" (Job 2:10).

Job's Friends

Job's three friends' theology was Deuteronomistic: God always blesses the righteous and punishes the wicked. Therefore, since Job was suffering and lost everything, he must have some hidden sin. It is interesting to note in this narrative, God declares that "Job suffered for no reason" so the moment a person devises a reason for Job's suffering, they place themselves back in the narrative and become like one of Job's friends, and at the conclusion of the narrative are rebuked by God.

As Deuteronomistic theologians, these three friends challenged Job's integrity and tried to uncover the source of Job's test. Instead of the general cause we live in a fallen world, therefore, we experience hardship, they believed there was a specific source such as Job had hidden sin or he displeased God. The rest of the narrative from chapters three through thirty-seven is Job's dialogue with his friends on the source of his trials and Job's personal defense. Chapters thirty-eight through forty-two conclude the narrative with God's response and Job's vindication. The book of Job amazingly never answers the reason God allowed Job to suffer but instead offers hope and restoration in eternity.

Message of Job

The main message of Job is not why there is suffering and evil but how will we respond? Job's response was both faith and trust and he said, "But God knows the way that I take; when He has tested me, I will come forth as gold" (Job 23:10). Tests and trials reveal who we really are and of what our faith is composed.

Job 38:1 and 40:6 says, "Then the Lord answered Job out of the storm." God spoke to Job through his dark storm and revealed Himself to him. Job responded to God's presence by stating, "My ears had heard of you (theology) but now my eyes have seen you (experience)" (Job 42:5). Job's trials gave him a greater understanding of God's character. Rabbi Abraham Heschel said, "Faith and character like Job's cannot be shaken because it is the result of having been shaken."

After Job prayed and interceded for his three friends the Lord restored back to him double of everything he had. Job 42:12-13 says, "The Lord blessed the latter part of Job's life more than the first. He had fourteen thousand sheep, six thousand camels, a thousand yoke of oxen and a thousand donkeys. And he also had seven sons and three daughters."

Job only received seven sons and three daughters, the same number that he had before. Why were they not doubled (Job 1:2, 42:13)? The reason Job received only seven sons and three daughters is unlike his livestock and earthly wealth, Job never lost them since they are in heaven. Thus from an eternal perspective Job even received twice the amount of children, only seven of his sons and three of his daughters are on earth and the others waiting for him in heaven.

In *A History of Heaven*, Professor Jeffrey Burton Russell wrote, "St. Augustine insisted that the paradise at the end of time is a *reformatio in melius*: it will restore, yet be superior to, that at the beginning of time. In the first paradise we had freedom to sin or not to sin, but in the eternal paradise we are so wedded to God that we lack even the ability to sin."[81]

Even the agents and source of Job's trials represent the tripolarity theory. The Sabeans' and Chaldeans' raiders (human agent) that killed Job's servants and plundered his livestock did so by their own

---

[81] Jeffrey Burton Russell, *A History of Heaven* (Princeton: Princeton University Press, 1997), 85.

free will. The pathogen inflicted on Job causing his sores was administered by Satan but also a result of the fall—sickness (devil's agent). God gave permission to Satan and removed His hedge of protection (divine agent). In Job's trials, God was in complete control and nothing happened outside His providence. As Job 42:2 states, "Lord I know you can do all things; no plan of yours can be thwarted."

Our Response

Jeremiah 14:8-9, written to a people in captivity, says, "O Hope of Israel, its Savior in times of distress, why are you like a stranger in the land, like a traveler who stays only a night? Why are you like a man taken by surprise, like a warrior powerless to save? You are among us, O Lord, and we bear your name; do not forsake us!" In this fallen world, sometimes we are like the weeping Prophet Jeremiah and his people in exile, feeling forsaken by God or our tragedy has taken even the Lord by surprise. Our response is trust and obedience realizing this earth is not our home. Job said, "Though he slay me, yet will I hope in him; I will surely defend my ways to his face" (Job 13:15).

Summary

God created an amazing world without sin. Due to the fall, we now experience suffering and death. Rachel, who died in a car accident her freshman year of college, during her senior year of high school posted on the wisdom tree (the senior high class's parting wisdom), "You can be anything you want in life, a doctor, an astronaut, teacher, business person, but just remember to love God every second of the day!" That's our response to a fallen world infested with cancer, car crashes, natural disasters, and wars; love and trust God, and be His agent of healing.

Chapter 11
Incarnation

The Word became flesh and theologians made it the word again.

Karl Barth

Christianity is the out-dwelling of the indwelling Christ.

C. I. Scofield

For in Christ all the fullness of the Deity lives in bodily form, and you have been given fullness in Christ, who is the head over every power and authority.

Colossians 2:9-10

And confessedly great is the mystery of godliness who was manifested in flesh, vindicated in spirit, seen by angels, preached among Gentiles, believed on in the world, and lifted up in glory.

1 Timothy 3:16

Introduction

GOD MAY THUNDER His Ten Commandments from Mount Sinai with lightning and people may tremble and be terrified, yet remain at heart exactly as they were before, unchanged and indifferent. Let a man or woman see their God down in the arena as a man, working hard labor with callused hands as an obscure carpenter, suffering, tempted, and sweating as we also are in life—finally dying a criminal's death on a Roman cross, and he or she is a hard-hearted person indeed who is untouched and without tears.[82] The incarnation is the price God paid to redeem us.

Ministry of Jesus

Jesus' ministry was threefold: teaching, preaching, and healing. Matthew 4:23 states, "Jesus went throughout Galilee, teaching in their synagogues, preaching the good news of the kingdom, and healing every disease and sickness." The message Jesus taught was the Kingdom of God. The Kingdom of God is God's presence, authority, and influence manifested on earth. Jesus' ministry embodies the Kingdom of God through His incarnation.

In Mark's gospel Jesus has power over all forces, so no matter the problem, Jesus is the answer. Jesus calms the Sea of Galilee, demonstrating He has authority over nature; He expels demons, proving His authority over the supernatural realm; He heals the woman with the issue of blood for twelve years, thus He has authority over sickness; and finally He raises Jairus's daughter from the dead (Mark 4:35-5:43).

The tripolarity theory in the incarnation is seen by Jesus' ministry. Jesus' preaching and teaching demands a response on the behalf of His hearers; this is the human agent of choice. The Holy Spirit empowered Jesus and guided Him, the agent of God. Christ expelled demons and destroyed the kingdom of Satan, thus the agent of the devil.

Seven Jewish Feasts

The Scriptures teach that Jesus fulfilled all the laws and the prophets. Luke wrote, "Jesus said, 'This is what I told you while I was still with you: Everything must be fulfilled that is written about me in the Law of Moses, the Prophets and the Psalms'" (Luke 24:44). The Jews

---

[82] J.B. Phillips, *Your God Is Too Small* (New York: Macmillan Company, 1961), 109.

celebrated seven major feasts: Passover, Unleavened Bread, Firstfruits, Pentecost, Trumpets, Day of Atonement, and Tabernacles.

The Feast of Passover commemorated the Israelites' deliverance from the bondage of Egypt. Christ fulfilled this feast with the Last Supper and the New Covenant in His blood. Jesus in the upper room gave His disciples the cup and said, "This is my blood of the new covenant, which is poured out for many" (Mark 14:24).

The Feast of Unleavened Bread symbolized the hardship of Egypt and the purging of sin from the camp. Christ as the Lamb of God has taken away the sins of His people (John 1:29). Hebrews 13:12-13 says, "And so Jesus also suffered outside the city gate to make the people holy through his own blood. Let us, then, go to him outside the camp, bearing the disgrace he bore."

On the Feast of Firstfruits, Israel brought the firstfruits of the harvest into the Lord's house to acknowledge God as their source. Jesus rose from the dead on this feast, demonstrating He is the firstfruit of the resurrection. 1 Corinthians 15:20 says, "But now Christ has been raised from the dead the firstfruits of those who have fallen asleep."

The Feast of Pentecost represented the day of harvest. The Holy Spirit was given to the hundred and twenty in the upper room on Pentecost (Acts 2:1-13). As Jesus departed, He commanded His disciples, "I am going to send you what my Father has promised; but stay in the city until you have been clothed with power from on high" (Luke 24:49).

During the Feast of Trumpets the priest blows the horn declaring the beginning of a new year. In the synagogues Isaiah 60-61 is read declaring the Lord reigns on the earth. In Luke's gospel, Jesus began his public ministry on this date by reading Isaiah 61:1-2 in the local synagogue (Luke 4:17-21).

On the Day of Atonement the high priest entered the Holy of Holies and made atonement for the sins of the people. Jesus' death on the cross removed the wall of separation and gave us access to the presence of God. Matthew 27:52 says, "At that moment the curtain of the temple was torn in two from top to bottom. The earth shook and the rocks split."

The final feast was the Feast of Tabernacles, commemorating the Israelites wandering in the wilderness and God's presence following them for those forty years. This feast was fulfilled by the incarnation and Jesus' birth on the Feast of Tabernacles. John wrote in his prologue, "The Word became flesh and made his dwelling among us. We have seen his glory, the glory of the One and Only, who came from the Father, full of grace and truth" (John 1:14). The word translated "dwelling" is εσκηνωσεν and means "to settle or live in a tent" and is used for the Feast of Tabernacle in the LXX translation. Raymond Brown states, "The flesh of Jesus is the new localization of God's presence on earth; Jesus is the replacement of the ancient tabernacle."[83]

Year of Jubilee

Jesus began his public ministry in the year of Jubilee to set the captives free. Every fiftieth year was a Jubilee and during this year, every Jewish slave was freed, every prisoner released, all debts were cancelled, and each Jew returned to their own family property (Leviticus 25).

The Birth of Jesus

The birth narrative account in Matthew's gospel reveals Christ's threefold office as king, priest, and the atonement sacrifice. Matthew 2:11 states, "On coming to the house, the Magi saw the child with his mother Mary, and they bowed down and worshipped him. Then they opened their treasures and presented him with gifts of gold and of incense and of myrrh."

---

[83] Raymond Brown, *The Epistle of John. The Anchor Bible.* (Garden City: Doubleday, 1982), 502.

King

The gold demonstrates Jesus' kingship. Jesus came as the sacrificial lamb, but at His return, will come as the lion of the tribe of Judah. In the incarnation, Jesus came humbly on a donkey into Jerusalem, but at His return triumphantly on a white horse (Matt. 21:7; Rev. 19:11).

Adam Hamilton wrote, "What kind of King was Jesus? He is a King who rode into Jerusalem on a donkey, was anointed by a prostitute, was crowned with thorns, and was enthroned when he hung on a cross, so that you and I might know the love and mercy of God, accept it, and follow him."[84]

Priest

The Magi's gift of incense reveals Jesus is a priest who intercedes on behalf of His people. The book of Hebrews tells us that Jesus is our high priest who makes atonement for our sins. Christ's blood is what redeems our lives from the law and sin. The Magi's greatest gift was the myrrh because it symbolized Jesus' death on the cross that brought salvation.

Atonement Sacrifice

The myrrh revealed Jesus' mission on earth was to die as an atoning sacrifice for sin. 1 John 4:10 says, "This is love: not that we loved God, but that he loved us and sent his Son as an atoning sacrifice for our sins."

Temptation of Christ

Matthew 4:1-4 states, "Then Jesus was led by the Spirit into the desert to be tempted by the devil. After fasting forty days and forty nights, he was hungry. The tempter came to him and said, 'If you are the Son of God, tell these stones to become bread.' Jesus answered, 'It is

---

[84] Adam Hamilton, *The Way: Walking in the Footsteps of Jesus* (Nashville: Abingdon Press, 2012), 158.

written: "Man does not live on bread alone, but on every word that comes from the mouth of God.""'"

The temptation of Jesus demonstrates the tripolarity theory and locus of control is internal and external: Jesus was tempted by the devil (external), Jesus was hungry from fasting forty days (internal, free choice to transform stones into bread), and God is the One who empowered Jesus to overcome the temptation (external). The Spirit led Jesus into the desert to be tempted, the devil tempted Christ, and He was hungry from fasting in His humanity. Jesus overcame the devil's temptation by the word of God. The word of God is the truth combating against the devil's arsenal of deception (John 17:17).

Power of the Kingdom

Jesus' response to His divine authority was humility and submission to the Father. Philippians 2:6-11 states,

> "Who being in very nature God, did not consider equality with God something to be grasped, but made himself nothing, taking the very nature of a servant, being made in human likeness. And being found in appearance as a man, he humbled himself and became obedient to death—even death on a cross! Therefore God exalted him to the highest place and gave him the name that is above every name, that at the name of Jesus every knee should bow, in heaven and on earth and under the earth, and every tongue confess that Jesus Christ is Lord, to the glory of God the Father."

Christ humbled Himself to the lowest point, death on the cross; God exalted Him to the highest above the heavens and caused all creation to bow before Him in reverence. The devil exalted himself to the highest place in heaven and God brought him down to the lowest hell (Isaiah 14:11-16). C.S. Lewis observed: "The higher a thing is, the lower it can descend."[85] Humility is the key to authority in God's kingdom. John the Baptist said in reference to Jesus' ministry expanding, "He must become greater; I must become less" (John 3:30). St. Augustine said, "Only through humbling oneself does one come into the glory of the Lord."

Divine Nature

The biblical writers describe Jesus as having all the attributes of God. Jesus is omnipotent—all-powerful (Matt. 28:18), omniscient—all-knowing (John 21:17), omnipresent—ever-present (Matt. 28:20), immutable—unchanging in His divine nature (Heb. 13:8), eternal—from the beginning (John 1:2). In the incarnation some of these divine metaphysical attributes were limited by Christ's humanity, such as omniscience (Matt. 24:36), omnipresence (John 11:21), and immutability (Luke 8:46).

When Jesus cried out on the cross, "My God, my God, why have you forsaken me?" Jesus was quoting Psalm 22:1 and the absence of God's tangible presence in the moment of His despair. An example of the presence of God departing is in the narrative of the Ark of God being captured by the Philistines. 1 Samuel 4:22 states, "The glory has departed from Israel, for the ark of God has been captured."

Worshipped

Jesus received praise and worship as God. Matthew 14:33 says, "Then those who were in the boat worshipped Jesus, saying, 'Truly you are the Son of God.'" John 9:38 states, concerning the man who was healed by Jesus, "Then the man said, 'Lord, I believe,' and he worshipped him."

Trinity

The relationship between the Persons of the Trinity was described by early Christians as an eternal holy dance of each Person in the Trinity

---

[85] C. S. Lewis, *The Great Divorce* (New York: Macmillan, 1946), 124.

around and within the others. The Trinity in the incarnation is demonstrated by Jesus' baptism. Jesus is baptized, the Father spoke from heaven, and the Holy Spirit descended as a dove on Christ in perfect unity (Matt. 3:16-17).

Diabolic Counterfeit

The antichrist is the diabolic counterfeit to the incarnation. Satan, near the time of Christ's return, will indwell as a world ruler and through this ruler establish a one-world government and receive praise as a god.

This world ruler, "the man of Lawlessness," will exalt himself and his power over the kingdom of God. The Apostle Paul said, "Don't let anyone deceive you in any way, for that day will not come until the rebellion occurs and the man of lawlessness is revealed, the man doomed to destruction. He will oppose and exalt himself over everything that is called God or is worshipped, so that he sets himself up in God's temple, proclaiming himself to be God" (2 Thess. 2:4-5).

Every generation has a form of an antichrist. An antichrist is anyone who opposes God. 1 John 4:3 says, "Every spirit that does not acknowledge Jesus is not from God. This is the spirit of antichrist, which you have heard is coming and even now is already in the world." G. C. Berkouwer states, "In eschatology one must distinguish between 'forerunners' (antichrists) and the antichrist. The 'antichrists' are present with us; the 'antichrist' will appear at the end of history. In this sense the antichrist's influence is present throughout history; but one day these powers will be embodied in one kingdom of the world, the apotheosis of apostasy."[86]

Anthony A. Hoekema wrote, "We may say that every age will provide its own particular form of antichristian activity. But we look

---

[86] G. C. Berkouwer, *The Return of Christ* (Grand Rapids: Eerdmans, 1972), 113-14.

for an intensification of this sign in the appearance of the antichrist shortly before Christ's return."[87]

For Daniel's Jewish audience in the second century the antichrist was Epiphanes IV Antiochus from the Seleucid Empire. He was a Greek tyrant who outlawed Judaism, killed 40,000 Jews, and desecrated their sacred temple with pigs. In Paul's letter the antichrists for his generation were the Caesars Nero and Caligula. The Apostle Paul foresaw a future antichrist that embodies all the evils of the previous ones and is Satan incarnate in the flesh. This antichrist will be a counterfeit Savior as Revelation 13:11 states, "Then I saw another beast, coming out of the earth. He had two horns like a lamb, but spoke like a dragon."

The Apostle John describes this final antichrist (the Beast) in Revelation 13:5-6, "The beast was given a mouth to utter proud words and blasphemies and to exercise his authority for forty-two months. He opened his mouth to blaspheme God, and his dwelling place and those who live in heaven." The beast was granted power to rule for seven years (a complete period of time) and midway through his reign he will break his peace treaty and begin a great persecution of the saints and the Jews.

The antichrist will be wounded and returned to life (Rev. 13:14).[88] It is interesting that all the former archetypes of antichrist are removed from power by God through their death, but the final antichrist has a pseudo-resurrection. Satan incarnates the antichrist and causes the antichrist's body to rise from the dead.

Jesus said, "For false Christs and false prophets will appear and perform great signs and miracles to deceive even the elect—if that were possible" (Matt. 24:24). Notice the text says 'Christs' in the plural meaning more than one pretend Messiah or antichrists.

---

[87] Anthony A. Hoekema, *The Bible and the Future* (Grand Rapids: Eerdmans, 1979), 162.

[88] After the death of Nero it was rumored he was raised from the dead; this was termed the Nero redivivus legend.

Revelation 16:13-14 states, "Then I saw three evil spirits that looked like frogs; they came out of the mouth of the dragon, out of the mouth of the beast and out of the mouth of the false prophet. They are the spirits of demons performing miraculous signs, and they go out to the kings of the world, to gather them for the battle on the great day of God Almighty." The unholy pseudo trinity is the dragon (Satan), the beast (antichrist) and the false prophet. Satan will receive worship and praise from unbelievers through the antichrist and the false prophet.

The question now arises if there have been many antichrists throughout history, who or what is holding back the appearing of the final antichrist, Satan incarnate in the flesh as the world ruler?

Antichrist's Appearing

As we have seen, there have been in history, many examples of antichrists from Nimrod and Pharaoh to the modern-era Hitler and Stalin. The Apostle Paul writes, "And now you know what is holding him (antichrist) back, so he may be revealed at the proper time. For the secret power of lawlessness is already at work; but the one who now holds it back will continue to do so till he is taken out of the way. And then the lawless one will be revealed, whom the Lord Jesus will overthrow with the breath of his mouth and destroy the splendor of his coming" (2 Thess. 2:6-8).

The appearing of the antichrist is held back with accordance to God's perfect timeline. The Apostle John in the seventeenth chapter of Revelation verse ten mentions that seven kings must first arise before the eighth king, the antichrist. The number seven is the number of perfection and in this text it symbolizes completion. Thus when the perfect time of God arrives, He allows Satan to be incarnate in the flesh.

Daniel writes, "He changes times and seasons; he sets up kings and deposes them. He gives wisdom to the wise and knowledge to the discerning" (Daniel 2:21). God is the one who appoints the times and seasons of world events, and with His providence establishes and deposes rulers. John mentions in Revelation 17:10 five of the kings have fallen; the five which had fallen were deposed by God so they were unable to wreak any further destruction upon the earth. Their untimely deaths prevented Satan from establishing a one-world government.

The sixth king, the one in power, during the writing of Revelation in 95/96 A.D. was Caesar Domitian whose reign of persecution resulted in over 40,000 Christian martyrs. The seventh king is the antichrist and he is raised from the dead thus becoming an eighth king. John writes, "The beast who once was, and now is not, is an eighth king. He belongs to the seven and is going to his destruction" (Rev. 17:11). Daniel 7:25 states, "He (antichrist) will speak against the Most High and oppress his saints and try to change the set times and the laws. The saints will be handed over to him for a time, times and half a time." Satan, through the different antichrists, attempts to gain world control and change the times appointed by God, but he is unsuccessful.

Tripolarity Theory

The tripolarity is seen in the antichrist by God choosing the time of the world ruler's reign and his defeat at Christ's return (God), by humanity giving their sovereign rule to the antichrist (free will) and Satan's incarnation in the antichrist (the devil). Revelation 17:13 says, "They (appointed governments) have one purpose and will give their power and authority to the beast." John said, "For God has put it into their hearts to accomplish his purpose by agreeing (free will) to give the beast their power to rule, until God's words are fulfilled" (Rev. 17:17).

Christ's Lordship

The Apostle Paul said, "For everyone who calls on the name of the Lord will be saved" (Rom. 10:13). The name Jesus (Yeshua) is derived from the common Hebrew name Joshua and means "Jehovah saves." Matthew 1:21 said, "She (Mary) will give birth to a son, and you are to give him the name Jesus, because he will save his people from their sins." Since the name Jesus means "God saves," if an unbeliever or a person who has never heard the gospel, in his dying breath calls forth, "God save me," they would be calling on the name of the Lord and God would usher them into His glorious kingdom.

The Bible teaches salvation is only in Christ and faith in Him. Jesus said, "I am the way and the truth and the life. No one comes to the Father except through me" (John 14:6). Acts 4:12 says, "Salvation is found in no one else, for there is no other name under heaven given to men by which we must be saved." Since Christ is the way, the truth, and the life, we must receive Jesus as our Lord and Savior. John writes, "Yet to all who received him, to those who believed in his name, he gave the right to become children of God—children born not of natural descent, nor of human decision or a husband's will, but born of God" (John 1:12-13).

Summary

Hebrews 12:2-3 says, "Let us fix our eyes on Jesus, the author and perfecter of our faith, who for the joy set before him endured the cross, scorning its shame, and sat down at the right hand of the throne of God. Consider him who endured such opposition from sinful men, so that you will not grow weary and lose heart." We are in a cosmic battle and Christ has empowered us to overcome by the power of His blood and the word of our testimonies. Let us live for Christ and discover our identity in Him. The Apostle Paul wrote, "For to me, to live is Christ and to die is gain" (Phil. 1:21).

Chapter 12
Eschatology

Heaven is a prepared place for a prepared people.

D. L. Moody

The first coming of Christ, God's Son and our God was in obscurity. The second will be in sight of the whole world.

St. Augustine

And then they will see the Son of Man coming in the clouds with great power and glory. And then He will send out the angles: and they will gather together His chosen ones from the four winds from the ends of the earth to the ends of the heavens.[89]

Mark 13:26-27

Be careful, or your hearts will be weighed down with carousing, drunkenness and the anxieties of life, and that day will close on you unexpectedly like a trap. For it will come upon all those who live on the face of the whole earth.

Luke 21:34-35

Introduction

THE FIRST COMING OF CHRIST was as a baby clothed in humanity, to die for our sins, the Suffering Servant; His second coming will be with power and glory as the risen Son of Man. The

---

[89] Ron Sandison's translation from Greek to English

One who appeared as the sacrificial lamb will return as the lion from the tribe of Judah. Hebrews 9:28 declares, "Christ was sacrificed once to take away the sins of many people; and he will appear a second time, not to bear sin, but to bring salvation to those who are waiting for him."

The Thessalonian community to whom Paul wrote his two epistles had a few misconceptions concerning Christ's return. Some Thessalonians believed Christ's return was immediate and therefore they should cease to work and just wait patiently. Paul warned these freeloader believers, "If a man will not work, he shall not eat" (2 Thess. 3:10). Other Thessalonians believed those who died prior to Christ's return would perish and not participate in the resurrection in the age to come. Paul encouraged these believers, "Christ died for us so that, whether we are awake or asleep, we may live together with him" (1 Thess. 5:10) and at Christ's return these believers who had already died will be with Him (1 Thess. 4:14-15).

The final pseudo-view held by some Thessalonians was Christ had already returned spiritually, not physically. 2 Thessalonians 2:1-2 says, "Concerning the coming of our Lord Jesus Christ and our being gathered to him, we ask you brothers, not to become easily unsettled or alarmed by some prophecy, report or letters supposed to have come from us, saying that the day of the Lord has already come." Paul instructs these misinformed believers that at Christ' return, Satan will be defeated and the whole world will see Jesus at His appearing (2 Thess. 2:8).

Second Coming

Christ revealed to His disciples in the Olivet Discourse the whole world will witness His return. Jesus said, "For as lightning that comes from the east is visible even in the west, so will be the coming of the Son of Man" (Matt. 24:27). After Jesus' resurrection and forty days appearing, as He ascended into heaven a cloud hid Him from His disciples. As the disciples looked into the sky at Christ's ascension, two angels appeared and said, "Men of Galilee, why do you stand here looking into the sky? This same Jesus, who has been taken from you into heaven, will come back in the same way you have seen him go into heaven" (Acts 1:10-11).

The biblical writers use three Greek words for Christ's return: παρουσια, επιφανεια, αποκαλυψις. Παρουσια means "arrival or coming" and was a term used for Caesar's return from a victory in battle. This word is used twenty-four times in the New Testament, seventeen of those with reference to Christ's return. It was also used for "the coming of the lawless one (antichrist)" demonstrating Satan's counterfeit savior (2 Thess. 2:9). Matthew 24:3 states, "As Jesus was sitting on the Mount of Olives, the disciples came to him privately. "Tell us," they said, "when will this happen, and what will be the sign of your coming (παρουσιας) and the end of the age?" James wrote, "Be patient, then, brothers until the Lord's coming (παρουσιας). See how the farmer waits for the land to yield its valuable crop and how patient he is for the autumn and spring rains" (Jam. 5:7). This is the most frequently used word for Jesus' return.

Επιφανεια is used five times concerning Christ's return and means "to appear, manifest, and a shining forth." When the Greeks believed they witnessed a miraculous intervention by the gods on their behalf they referred to the event as επιφανεια. 2 Timothy 4:1 says, "In the presence of God and of Christ Jesus, who will judge the living and the dead, and in view of his appearing (επιφανειαν) and his kingdom, I give you this charge."

The final word for Christ's return is αποκαλυψις and means "uncovering or unveiling, a revelation." This term was used in classic Greek when a sculptor removed a cloth from their statue to reveal their masterpiece. 1 Peter 4:13 says, "But rejoice that you participate in the sufferings of Christ, so that you may be overjoyed when his glory is revealed (αποκαλυψει). These three words demonstrate that Christ's second coming will be both visible and physical.

Eschatology

Eschatology, the study of last things, is derived from the Greek word εσχατος, meaning "last" and -logy, meaning "the study of." Revelation 1:17 states, "When I saw him, I fell at his feet as though dead. Then he placed his right hand on me and said: 'Do not be afraid. I am the First and the Last (εσχατος).'" As the book of Revelation demonstrates, eschatology is the study of end time events, the kingdom of God, and Christ's return. Walter Kaiser wrote, "An eschatology without Christology is like a book without a first and final chapter, for Jesus is the alpha and omega to all history and eschatology!"[90] Theologian Jürgen Moltmann said, "From first to last, and not merely in the epilogue, Christianity is eschatology, is hope, forward looking and forward moving, and therefore also revolutionizing and transforming the present."

Day & Hour Unknown

The time of Christ's return is unknown; therefore, we must be prepared. Clement in the first century preached, "Let us wait therefore, hour by hour for the kingdom of God in love and righteousness, since we do not know the day of Christ's appearing."

As the people in Noah's day did not know when the door on the ark would shut and the heavens gush forth rain, so we do not know when the clouds will break open to reveal Christ's return. 1 Thessalonians 5:1-2 states, "Now, brothers, about times and dates we do not need to write to you, for you know very well that the day of the Lord will come like a thief in the night."

Thieves come suddenly in the night and when we least expect them. If we knew when a thief was coming we would be prepared. Luke 12:38-40 states, "It will be good for those servants whose master finds them ready, even if he comes in the second or third watch of the night. But understand this: If the owner of the house had known

---

[90] Walter C. Kaiser Jr., *Preaching and Teaching the Last Things* (Grand Rapids: Baker Academic, 2011), 51.

at what hour the thief was coming, he would not have let his house be broken into. You also must be ready, because the Son of Man will come at an hour when you do not expect him." The Greek word translated "watch" does not simply mean "to look for" but "to be awake."

Prepared

We are prepared and ready by living as though Christ died yesterday, arose this morning, and is coming again tomorrow. Since Christ's return will be sudden and without warning we must always be ready to meet the Lord. Jesus' parables of the Talents and Ten Minas teach us that the best way to be ready for His return is to be using our gifts for His kingdom (Matthew 25:14-30; Luke 19:11-27). In the Parable of the Ten Minas, the king commanded his servants to occupy until he came again (Luke 19:13). The word "occupy" means "to practice, to carry on," or to get on with the business of the coming King.

A Bible student approached John Wesley and asked him, "What would you do if you knew Jesus would return tomorrow?" Wesley said, "I would work in my garden." The young man was shocked and asked, "Why would you work in your garden?" Wesley replied, "Every day I live as if Christ will return and tomorrow is my day to work in my garden." Dr. Jack Van Impe for his fiftieth anniversary made a T-shirt that read, "Perhaps Today!"

Christ's Return

The New Testament writers teach we are living in the last days. The term "last days" in the Scriptures refers to the time period between Christ's ascension into heaven and His return in glory. Last days include Christ's resurrection, transfiguration, the destruction of Jerusalem, Christ's ascension, and the Day of Pentecost. The term "day of the Lord" refers to God's judgment at His appearing. The Prophet Amos wrote, "Woe to you who long for the day of the Lord! Why do you long for the day of the Lord? That day will be darkness, not light" (Amos 5:18). Ezekiel prophesied, "For the day is near, the day of the Lord is near—a day of clouds, a time of doom for the nations" (Ezekiel 30:3).

The day of the Lord in the New Testament is when Christ returns to judge the world and set up His kingdom. Paul said, "And do this, understanding the present time. The hour has come for you to wake up from your slumber, because our salvation is nearer now than when we first believed. The night is nearly over; the day is almost here. So let us put aside the deeds of darkness and put on the armor of light" (Rom. 13:11-12).

The present time is the age of grace and service. 2 Corinthians 6:1-2 states, "As God's fellow workers we urge you not to receive God's grace in vain. For he says, 'In the time of my favor I heard you, and in the day of salvation I helped you.' I tell you, now is the time of God's favor, now is the day of salvation."

The Prophet Daniel in the Old Testament prophesied Christ's appearing as a distant future event: "In my vision at night I looked, and there before me was one like a Son of Man, coming with the clouds of heaven. He approached the Ancient of Days and was led into his presence" (Dan. 7:13). Daniel was commanded by God to seal up his visions until the time of the end (Daniel 12:9). God said, "But you, Daniel, close up and seal the words of the scroll until the time of the end. Many will go here and there to increase knowledge" (Daniel 12:4). The sign of the end in the Book of Daniel is a vast increase in knowledge. This increase in knowledge can be seen in history with the printing press, the industrial revolution, and the age of the internet.

The Apostle John viewed Christ's return not as a distant future event, but as imminent. In Revelation, the Apostle John was commanded by God not to seal the words of prophecy of his book, because the time is near (Rev. 22:10). The Greek word for "near" can also be translated "at hand."

Last Days

The Prophet Daniel in his interpretation of King Nebuchadnezzar's dream demonstrated the erosion and decay of nations until Christ's return. King Nebuchadnezzar in his dream saw an enormous dazzling statue with a head of pure gold, chest and arms of silver, belly and thighs of bronze, legs of iron, and feet composed of iron mixed with clay (Dan. 2:31-45). In the dream the head of gold symbolized Babylon; the silver breastplates and arms—the Medes and Persians; the bronze groin—Greece under Alexander the Great; the iron legs—Rome; the cast iron and clay ten toes—the Revived Roman Empire.

The first three nations, Babylon, Medes, and Persians, and Greece are symbolized by rare precious metals and the final two kingdoms by common metals used for industry, demonstrating their corrosion and impurity. The Revived Roman Empire is the final corrupt kingdom before Christ's return—the antichrist will arise from this nation and bring destruction. Daniel prophesied in the future the Rock (Christ) will come and smash this final kingdom and then set up an eternal kingdom (Dan. 2:45).

Jesus taught before His return, the love of most will grow cold and lawlessness and wickedness will abound (Matt. 24:12). The devil in the tripolarity theory attempts to cause believers' love to grow cold and lose hope so they will not be prepared for Christ's return. Matthew 24:48-49 warns, "But suppose that servant is wicked and says to himself, 'My master is staying away a long time,' and he then begins to beat his fellow servants and to eat and drink with drunkards."

Delay in the παρουσια

Jesus predicted a delay in His return in the parables of the Ten Virgins and the Talents (Matt. 25:1-13; 25:12-30). Charles L. Holman said, "Half of the bridesmaids were caught off guard because they did not reckon with delay!"[91] This delay in Christ's return requires believers to stand firm in faith and not lose hope. Jesus' parable of the Unjust Judge demonstrates our need to persevere in faith as we wait for justice and Christ's return (Luke 18:1-8). This parable concludes with the statement, "I tell you, he (God) will see that they get justice, and quickly. However, when the Son of Man comes, will he find faith on the earth?" (Luke 18:8). The delay in Christ's return will cause the faith of some to grow weary and open to demonic attack (Luke 21:34).

The author of Hebrews predicted a delay and said, "So do not throw away your confidence; it will be richly rewarded. You need to persevere so that when you have done the will of God, you will receive what he has promised. For in just a very little while, "He who is coming will come and will not delay" (Heb. 10:35-37).

The Battle

The Apostle Paul taught a trumpet blast will herald the coming of the Lord with His followers (1 Thess. 4:16). The trumpet blast symbolized the cry for battle and readiness to attack. Joseph Plevnik wrote, "In the Dead Sea Scrolls the trumpet motif is a feature of the eschatological battle. This is a battle of the Qumran warriors and spiritual forces; God, his angels, and 'the sons of light' fight against Beliar, his hordes and the 'sons of darkness.'"[92] The New Testament employs the trumpet motif to depict the παρουσια in Matt. 24:31, 1 Cor. 15:52, and Rev. 11:15. 1 Corinthians 14:8 states, "If the trumpet does not sound a clear call, who will get ready for battle?"

We live between D-day and V-day. D-day was Christ's first coming, when the enemy was decisively defeated on Calvary which has guaranteed his final defeat. Jesus cried out on the cross, "It is finished!" (John 19:30) The Apostle Paul describes the devil's defeat at Calvary in Colossians 2:15, "And having disarmed the powers and

---

[91] Charles L. Holman, *Till Jesus Comes* (Peabody: Hendrickson, 1996), 122.
[92] Joseph Plevnik, *Paul and the Parousia* (Peabody: Hendrickson, 1997), 58.

authorities, he made a public spectacle of them, triumphing over them by the cross."

The second coming of Christ will be like V-day, in which the enemy finally lays down his arms and surrenders. This occurs at Christ's return when the devil and his followers are cast into the lake of fire (Rev. 20:10). Theologian Oscar Cullman said, "The hope of the final victory is so much the more vivid because of the unshakably firm conviction that the battle that decides the victory has already taken place."

As we wait for V-day (Christ's return) we have spiritual battles to fight. [93] Pastor Dominic Russo has a plaque in his office, "Give the devil a headache!" Christ's death on the cross not only gave the devil a permanent migraine, it made him a defeated foe. St. Anthony the Great said, "Since the Lord dwelt among us, the enemy has fallen, and his powers have been weakened. He does not submit quietly to his defeat but keeps on threatening like a tyrant. For our greatest weapon against them (demonic forces) is a right life and confidence in God."

Satan and his demons realize they are defeated and powerless before Christ and their destiny is the lake of fire. When Jesus expelled the demons from the man in the region of Gerasenes, the demons begged Christ not to order them to go into the abyss (Luke 8:31). The final state for those who reject Christ and follow the devil is an eternity separated from God. Matthew 25:41 states, "Then he will say to those on his left, 'Depart from me, you who are cursed, into the eternal fire prepared for the devil and his angels.'"

Now & Not Yet

The now and not yet side of faith in eschatology creates a tension as demonstrated by these theological truths. God promises us we are redeemed from the curse of the law in Christ and yet Christians still die by sickness and disease (Gal. 3:13). We have the power to live by

---

[93] See endnotes: D-day and V-day.

the Holy Spirit and yet we sometimes still sin by the flesh (Rom. 8). We are a new creation in Christ and yet we still allow the old man to make himself known (2 Cor. 5:17). We have been crucified with Christ and yet we still have fleshly desires (Rom. 7). The devil is defeated and yet he still sometimes leads us astray.

The now and not yet tension also exemplified by the New Testament concept of the Kingdom of God. We are in the kingdom and yet we look forward to its full manifestation; we share its blessing and yet await its total victory; we thank God for having brought us into His kingdom of the Son He loves and yet we continue to pray, "Thy kingdom come." The Kingdom of God involves two great moments, fulfillment within history and consummation at the end of history.

Prepare the Way of the Lord

The Pharisees and the Jewish religious leaders were unable to perceive Jesus as the Messiah because He did not come on a white horse; John the Baptist prepared His way in the spirit of Elijah and they were expecting the literal Prophet of Elijah. Ironically, the Jewish religious leaders were so ingrained by their dogmatic presuppositions that they demanded Pilate release Barabbas, a pseudo-messiah, rather than Jesus the true Messiah.

William J. Dumbrell wrote, "Jesus preaches that the breaking in of God's kingdom has begun, and he transforms the popular expectation of the kingdom of God, for the type of rule to which Jesus points differs markedly from popular supposition. For Jesus, God's concern for the underprivileged, the distressed, and the handicapped is a mark of the kingdom's entry."[94]

When Jesus healed a man who was blind from birth the Jewish leaders expelled the healed man from the synagogue. In response to their hard hearts, Jesus rebuked these religious leaders and

---

[94] William J. Dumbrell, *The Search for Order: Biblical Eschatology In Focus* (Grand Rapids: Baker, 1994), 187.

pronounced judgment on them. This narrative demonstrates that Jesus came for the outcast and not the self-righteous (John 9:1-41).

Matthew 21:43 states, "Therefore I tell you that the kingdom of God will be taken from you and given to a people who will produce its fruits." How can we not be like the religious leaders who missed experiencing Christ's first coming?

We find the answer in the examples of Simeon and Anna, who both bore fruit for God and served faithfully in the Holy Temple. Simeon and Anna, by the power of the Holy Spirit and His leading, recognized that Jesus was the Messiah to come and they were able to participate in the Kingdom of God. Luke writes,

> "Now there was a man in Jerusalem called Simeon, who was righteous and devout. He was waiting for the consolation of Israel, and the Holy Spirit was upon him. It had been revealed to him by the Holy Spirit that he would not die before he had seen the Lord's Christ. Moved by the Spirit, he went into the temple courts. When the parents brought in the child Jesus to do for him what the custom of the Law required, Simeon took him in his arms and praised God saying: 'Sovereign Lord, as you have promised, you now dismiss your servant in peace. For my eyes have seen your salvation, which you have prepared in the sight of all people, a light for revelation to the Gentiles and for the glory to your people Israel'" (Luke 2:25-32).

Simeon, unlike the religious leaders, was able to witness the Messiah Jesus because he was ready and led by the Holy Spirit. He served faithfully in the Temple as he waited for the coming Savior. Simeon's faith in God produced the fruit of righteousness and devotion. As Jesus' parents brought Him into the Temple to consecrate Him to the Lord, Simeon was sensitive to the Holy Spirit and able to perceive by divine revelation Jesus' true identity.

Anna demonstrated the qualities of readiness and preparation for the Messiah. She was a godly woman known for her faithful prayers and worship. Luke writes,

> "There was also a prophetess, Anna, the daughter of Phanuel, of the tribe of Asher. She was very old; she had lived with her husband seven years after her marriage, and then was a widow until she was eighty-four. She never left the temple but worshipped night and day, fasting and praying. Coming up to them at that very moment, she gave thanks to God and spoke about the child to all who were looking forward to redemption of Jerusalem" (Luke 2:36-38).

Anna's devotion and heart for the Lord enabled her to witness Christ's first coming. She worshipped day and night in the Temple. The Scriptures teach us that we must pray as Christ's return draws near (Matt. 24:20; Luke 18:1, 21:36; 1 Peter 4:7). Simeon and Anna were ready for the coming Savior by their fruitful service and the power of the Holy Spirit.

Free Will

Christ's return will bring salvation to the believers and judgment to the rebellious. Church Father Clement of Rome wrote, "For I myself am utterly sinful and dependent on God and have not yet escaped from temptation; but even though I am surrounded by the tools of the devil, I make every effort to pursue righteousness, that I may succeed in at least getting close to it, because I fear the coming judgment and wrath of God."

In Mark's gospel the phrase "coming of the Son of Man" represents deliverance and judgment (Mark 13:26). The judgment side is expressed when Jesus was on trial before the high priest. Mark writes, "Again the high priest asked him, 'Are you the Christ, the Son of the Blessed One?' 'I am,' said Jesus. 'And you will see the Son of Man sitting at the right hand of the Mighty One and coming with the clouds of heaven'" (Mark 14:61-62). The high priest saw the judgment of the coming of the Son of Man with the destruction of Jerusalem in 70 A.D.

This judgment theme is heightened by the fact that it occurred on the Jewish holiday Tisha B'Av—the exact same day the first temple in Jerusalem was destroyed in 586 B.C., though in years widely spread apart. C.E.B. Cranfield wrote, "There is a correspondence between the ruin of Jerusalem with its temple and the end of the age; the eschatological is seen as it were through the medium of an approaching historical crisis, the historical catastrophe being regarded as foreshadowing the final convulsion."[95]

The destruction of Jerusalem was the precursor of God's wrath, which will come to consummation with the tribulation, and Christ's return, when all the dead will be judged. According to Josephus, more than 1,462,000 people died during the destruction of Jerusalem. This is a minuscule number compared to the number who will die during the tribulation hour. Jesus said, "I tell you, on that night two people will be in one bed; one will be taken and the other left" (Luke 17:34). Jesus in this verse predicted that one out of every two people will die during the great tribulation. There are currently more than seven billion people on earth; if the tribulation began today more than three and a half billion souls would perish.

The salvation of the coming of the Son of Man is reserved only for the believers. God promises us when the Son of Man comes He will gather together all His faithful servants (Mark 13:27). The coming of the Son of Man will be so glorious for the saints, the sun and moon will lose their light compared to the radiance and brightness of Christ's glory.

Every one of us will see the coming of the Son of Man either as our Savior and Lord, which will be a glorious experience, or like the high priest who saw the judgment and wrath of God. We have a choice and free will to follow Christ and enter His kingdom or reject Him and experience the terror of an eternity without God.

---

[95] C.E.B. Cranfield, *The Gospel According to St. Mark*. CGT Commentary (Cambridge University, 1959), SJT 6:297

The Bible declares when Christ returns every knee will bow before Him in heaven and on earth and everyone will confess His Lordship (Phil 2:10-11). The writer of Hebrews says, "It is a dreadful thing to fall into the hands of the living God" (Heb. 10:31). John writes, "For God did not send his Son into the world to condemn the world, but to save the world through him" (John 3:17).

During the latter days of the Roman Empire Constantine established Christianity as the state religion. Julian, a cousin of Constantine, was a hypocrite and wanted the Roman Empire to return to its pagan roots. He was taught by the great church historian Eusebius, who later would call him Julian the Apostate. In Julian's heart he rejected the faith and when he became the emperor in 363 A.D., he did everything in his power to try and eradicate Christianity. He burned sacrifices to the gods morning and evening. Julian shook his dagger at the sky and called Jesus the Pale Galilean. His reign was only eighteen months. Finally he was dying in a battlefield in Persia and grabbed some of his own blood and he held it up, and with his last breath said, "You have conquered, oh Galilean!" Ironically Julian was buried in Tarsus, the hometown of the Apostle Paul, the man he hated second only to Jesus Christ. Jesus will conquer us either with His love and mercy or His wrath and judgment. Today let us repent of our sins and make Jesus the Lord of our lives.

Summary

In the tripolarity theory and eschatology, Christ will return to set up His kingdom and redeem His people. At Christ's return the earth will be restored from the effects of the fall and the curse in the Garden of Eden. The dead in Christ will be resurrected to eternal life and reign with Him forever. The devil and his fallen angels, along with those who rejected God, will be banished to the lake of fire. In view of eschatology and the tripolarity theory we have a mission to preach the gospel to all nations and make disciples (Matt. 28:19). Revelation 22:20 states, "Amen. Come, Lord Jesus."

Endnotes

THESE NOTES ARE PROVIDED to expand the points made in the chapters and are a helpful aid for future research on the topics, philosophies, and ideas presented in this book.

Introduction

St. Augustine of Hippo (354-430 A.D.) was bishop of Hippo and a voluminous writer on philosophical, exegetical, theological, and ecclesiological topics. He formulated the Western doctrines of predestination and original sin in his writings against the Pelagians.

St. Augustine authored *The City of God* and *On Free Choice of the Will* (*De Libero Arbitrio*); these writings' theologies contain the concept of the tripolarity theory. After the Pelagianism controversy on free will, St. Augustine's theological writings were based heavily on the doctrine of predestination and the foreknowledge of God. St. Augustine, in response to Pelagianism, taught salvation is received solely through an irresistible gift, the efficacious grace of God, but this was a gift one had a free choice to accept or refuse. He wrote two books combating semi-Pelagian doctrines titled *De Praedstinatione Sanctorum* (On the Predestination of the Saints) and *De Dono Perseverantiae* (On the Gift of Perseverance).

St. Augustine stated, "The conclusion is that we are by no means under compulsion to abandon free choice in favor of divine knowledge, nor we deny—God forbid!—that God knows the future, as a condition for holding free choice" (*City of God 5:10*).

Caravaggio's character and reputation: Contemporary author Jonathan Harr gives this historical description of the Italian Baroque artist: "Caravaggio was a genius, a revolutionary painter, and a man beset by personal demons. Four hundred years ago, he drank and brawled in the taverns and streets of Rome, moving from one rooming house to another, constantly in and out of jail, all the while painting works of transcendent emotional and visual power. He rose from obscurity to fame and wealth, but success didn't alter his violent temperament. His rage finally led him to commit murder, forcing him to flee Rome, a hunted man. He died young, alone, and under strange circumstances."

Holy Spirit

Professor Craig S. Keener wrote, "Imagine visiting a town at night that appears to have no lights, no televisions—not even alarm clocks. And then imagine learning that the town's power supply is virtually infinite, but that no one in the town had thought to turn any of their electrical appliances on. Wouldn't that town seem like a silly place to you? Yet the Church is all too often like that town. God has given us the power of His Holy Spirit to fulfill His mission in the world, yet few Christians have even begun to depend on His power."[96]

Hidden God

St. Augustine's definition of a miracle: Rollins Professor of History at Princeton University Peter Brown wrote, "A 'miracle' for Augustine was just such a reminder of the bounds imposed on the mind by habit. In a universe in which all processes happen by the will of God, there need be nothing less remarkable in the slow, habitual processes of nature. We take for granted the slow miracle by which water in the irrigation of a vineyard becomes wine: it is only when Christ turns water into wine, 'in quick motion' as it were, that we are amazed." [97]

---

[96] Craig S. Keener, *The Gift and Giver: the Holy Spirit for Today* (Grand Rapids: Baker Academic, 2001), 52.

[97] Peter Brown, *Augustine of Hippo: A Biography, new edition* (Berkeley and Los Angeles: University of California Press, 1967, 2000), 420.

Love of God

Detection of idols in our heart: The three questions we need to ask to detect idols in our heart; 1. Am I willing to sin to get it? 2. Am I willing to sin if I think I'm going to lose it? 3. Do I run to it for refuge instead of to God?

Origin of the Devil

In the New Testament there are 568 references to the devil and demons as compared, for example, to 340 to the Holy Spirit and 604 to miracles.

Morning Star: Myra B. Nagel wrote, "Both Morning Star and Dawn were names of Canaanite gods, and the "mount of assembly on the heights Zaphon" in Isaiah 14:13 was a mountain where the gods assembled. In a Canaanite myth, Attar the Morning Star tried to take the place of the god Baal. When his attempt failed, Attar was forced to come down from heaven and rule on earth. Isaiah's reference to the Morning Star is a part of a long taunting song directed to Babylon."[98]

Insidious Operation of the Devil: Part 1

Judas Iscariot's motive in the Gospel of Matthew for betraying Christ: Professor Bart D. Ehrman wrote concerning Judas Iscariot's motive in the Gospel of Matthew, "The motivation of greed fits in with Matthew's broader agenda in telling the story of Jesus. In Matthew's earlier account of Jesus' teaching, not found in Mark, Jesus had stressed the importance of being more concerned with having treasure in heaven than on earth; he had taught them not to be concerned about the material things of this world; he had told them that it was impossible to serve both God and riches. He had also taught them that they should treat others as they wanted to be treated themselves. In Matthew's version of Jesus' arrest, not only does Judas betray his master, but in doing so he shows that he stands

---

[98] Myra B. Nagel, *Deliver Us from Evil* (Cleveland: United Church Press, 1999), 13.

completely against everything Jesus stood for. He was more interested in earthly treasure, in material things, in riches. And he certainly was not treating Jesus in the way he himself would have wanted to be treated. Matthew's Judas is the negative example of discipleship."

Insidious Operation of the Devil: Part 2

William J. Murray attributed his mother's atheism to anger, not intellectual conviction. William stated, "She felt two men had wronged her. Madalyn was mad at men, and she was mad at God, who made them."

Madalyn's son Garth's only friend was a churchgoing Christian named Mike.

Perception and Choice

John List's explanation for murdering his family: John List in his autobiography/personal memoirs *Collateral Damage* blamed post-traumatic stress disorder (PTSD) as the main contributing factor to his murdering his whole family. He claimed that he had PTSD from his forty-one days of combat in Germany as an infantryman in World War II and his being captured by the Germans and held as a prisoner of war.[99]

It is ironic that Austin Goodrich, the coauthor of *Collateral Damage*, had many things in common with John List; both were raised in Michigan, graduated from University of Michigan in 1949, served in the same 86th Blackhawk Division platoon for 30 months in World War II, and both used aliases to conceal their true identity. Goodrich went undercover as a CIA officer, while List was undercover to escape the law after he murdered his family in 1971. What caused John List to become a calculated cold-blooded murderer and Austin Goodrich a successful CIA officer? Could it be their different perceptions and choices in life?

---

[99] John List with Austin Goodrich, *Collateral Damage: the John List Story* (New York: iUniverse, Inc., 2006), 23.

Growth

Self-determined people know how to choose. They know what they want and how to get it. From an awareness of personal needs, self-determined individuals choose goals, then doggedly pursue them. This involves asserting an individual's presence, making his or her needs known, evaluating progress toward meeting goals, adjusting performance, and creating unique approaches to solve problems.

Creation

Lee Strobel, author of *The Case for a Creator*, wrote, "I realized that if I were to embrace Darwinism and its underlying premise of naturalism, I would have to believe that: 1. Nothing produces everything 2. Non-life produces life. 3. Randomness produces fine-tuning. 4. Chaos produces information. 5. Unconsciousness produces consciousness. 6. Non-reason produces reason. Based on this, I was forced to conclude that Darwinism would require a blind leap of faith that I was not willing to make."[100]

Christian philosopher Francis A. Schaeffer argued against atheism with the presupposition statement, "And no-one has shown how time plus chance can produce a qualitative change from impersonal to personal."[101]

Three main traditional views of evil: 1. Metaphysical evil, the lack of perfection inherent in any created world. 2. Natural evil, the suffering that comes from acts of nature such as cancers and tornadoes. 3. Moral evil, the deliberate willingness to inflict suffering.

The Fall

Philip Yancey said, "Grace is the most perplexing, powerful force in the universe, and, I believe, the only hope for our twisted, violent planet."

---

[100] Lee Strobel, *The Case for a Creator* (Grand Rapids: Zondervan, 2004), 277.
[101] Francis A. Schaeffer, *Escape from Reason* (Downers Grove: Inter-Varsity, 1978), 87.

Incarnation

Different presuppositions of Christ and the actions they produce: "Jesus is dangerous, let's oppose Him. He's a criminal, let's execute Him. Christ's divine, let's follow Him and worship Him."

Eschatology

D-day and V-day: Theologian John Marsh gives the following illustration that demonstrates D-day and V-day, which he himself heard from Bishop Nygren: "Hitler had occupied Norway, but in 1942 it was liberated. Suppose that up in the almost inaccessible north some small village with a Nazi overlord failed to hear the news of the liberation for some weeks. During that time, we might put it, the inhabitants of the village were living in the 'old' time of Nazi occupation instead of the 'new' time of Norwegian liberation… Any person who now lives in a world that has been liberated from the tyranny of evil powers either in ignorance of, or in indifference to, what Christ has done, is precisely in the position of those Norwegians to whom the good news of deliverance failed to penetrate. It is quite easy for us to see men can live B.C. in A.D."[102]

Anthony A. Hoekema wrote, "The greatest eschatological event in history is not in the future but in the past. Since Christ has won a decisive victory over Satan, sin, and death in the past, future eschatological events must be seen as the completion of a redemptive process which has already begun. What will happen on the last day, in other words, will be but the culmination of what has been happening in these last days."[103]

---

[102] John Marsh, *The Fulness of Time* (London: Nisbet, 1952), 155-156.

[103] Anthony A. Hoekema, *The Bible and the Future* (Grand Rapids: Eerdmans Publishing, 1979), 77.

Bibliography

Aquinas, Thomas. *Summa Theological*. New York: Echo Library, 2007.

Athanasius, Saint. *On the Incarnation: the Treatise De Incarnatione Verbi Dei*; translated and edited by a Religious of C.S.M.V. Crestwood: St. Vladimir's Seminary Press, 1996.

Augustine, Saint. *Confessions*; translated by Henry Chadwick. Oxford: Oxford University Press, 1991.

Augustine, Saint. *On Free Choice of the Will*; translated by A.S. Benjamin and L. H. Hackstaff. Indianapolis: The Bobbs-Merrill Co., 1964.

Augustine, Saint. *The City of God*; translated by Vernon J. Bourke. New York: Image, 1958.

Ayres, Lewis. *Augustine and the Trinity*. Cambridge: Cambridge University Press, 2010.

Barth, Karl. *God Here and Now*; translated by Paul M. Van Buren. New York and Evanston: Harper & Row Publishers, 1964.

Beamer, Lisa with Abraham, Ken. *Let's Roll!* Grand Rapids: Zondervan, 2002.

Benford, Timothy B. and Johnson, James P. *Righteous Carnage: the List Murders in Westfield*. New York: Charles Scribner's Sons, 1991.

Berkouwer, G.C. *The Return of Christ*. Grand Rapids: Eerdmans, 1972.

Bevere, John. *Extraordinary*. Colorado Springs: WaterBrook Press, 2009.

Bevere, John. *Relentless*. Colorado Springs: WaterBrook Press, 2011.

Boettner, Loraine. *The Reformed Doctrine of Predestination*, 8th edition. Grand Rapids: Eerdmans, 1958.

Bonhoeffer, Dietrich. *The Cost of Discipleship*. New York: Touchstone, 1959.

Boyd, Gregory A. *Satan and the Problem of Evil*. Downers Grove: InterVarsity, 2001.

Brandon, S.G.F. *Jesus and the Zealots: A Study of the Political Factor in Primitive Christianity*. Manchester: Manchester University Press, 1967.

Brown, Peter, *Augustine of Hippo: A Biography*, new edition with an Epilogue. Berkeley and Los Angeles: University of California Press, 1967, 2000.

Brown, Raymond. *The Epistle of John. The Anchor Bible*. Garden City: Doubleday, 1982.

Carus, Paul. *The History of the Devil and the Idea of Evil*. New York: Gramercy Books, 1996.

Chambers, Oswald. *My Utmost for His Highest*. Uhrichsville: Barbour Publishing, 1935.

Charlesworth, James H. *The Good & Evil Serpent: How a Universal Symbol Became Christianized*. New Haven: Yale University Press, 2010.

Crabb, Larry. *Finding God*. Grand Rapids: Zondervan, 1993.

Cranfield, C.E.B. *The Gospel According to St. Mark. CGT Commentary*. Cambridge University, 1959.

Dracos, Ted. *Ungodly: the Passions, Torments, and Murder of Atheist Madalyn Murray O'Hair*. New York: Free Press, 2003.

Dumbrell, William J. *The Search for Order: Biblical Eschatology in Focus*. Grand Rapids: Baker Books, 1994.

Ehrman, Bart D. *Lost Christianities*. New York: Oxford Press, 2003.

Erickson, Millard J. *Introducing Christian Doctrine* Grand Rapids: Baker Books, 1992.

Forsyth, Neil. *The Old Enemy: Satan & the Combat Myth*. Princeton: Princeton University Press, 1987.

Gladwell, Malcolm. *Outliers: the Story of Success*. New York: Little Brown, 2008.

Hamilton, Adam. *The Way: Walking in the Footsteps of Jesus*. Nashville: Abingdon Press, 2012.

Harrison, Carol. *Augustine: Christian Truth and Fractured Humanity*. New York: Oxford University Press, 2000.

Harrison, Carol. *Beauty and Revelation in the Thought of Saint Augustine*. Oxford: Clarendon, 1992.

Harrison, Carol. *Rethinking Augustine's Early Theology: An Argument for Continuity*. New York: Oxford University Press, 2006.

Hart, David Bentley. *The Doors of the Sea: Where was God in the Tsunami?* Grand Rapids: Eerdmans, 2005.

Heeren, Fred. *Show Me God*, Wonders Vol. 1. Wheeling: Day Star Publications, fourth printing, 1998.

Hoekema, Anthony A. *The Bible and the Future*. Grand Rapids: Eerdmans Publishing, 1979.

Holman, Charles L. *Till Jesus Comes*. Peabody: Hendrickson Publishers, 1996.

Jastrow, Robert. *God and the Astronomers*, second edition. New York: W.W. Norton & Company, 1992.

Johnson, Luke Timothy. *Living Jesus*. New York: HarperCollins, 1990.

Kaiser, Walter C. *Preaching and Teaching the Last Things*. Grand Rapids: Baker Academic, 2011.

Keener, Craig S. *Gift and Giver: the Holy Spirit for Today*. Grand Rapids: Academic, 2001.

Lehrer, Jonah. *How We Decide*. New York: Mariner Books, 2009.

Lessing, Gotthold Ephraim. *Lessing's Theological Writings*; translated by Henry Chadwick Stanford University Press, 1957.

Levering, Matthew. *The Theology of Augustine: An Introductory Guide to His Most Important Works*. Grand Rapids: Baker Academic, 2013.

Lewis, C.S. *The Great Divorce*. New York: Macmillan, 1964.

Lewis, C.S. *The Problem of Pain*. New York: Macmillan, 1962.

Lightfoot, J.B. and J.R. Harmer, editors and translators. *The Apostolic Fathers: Greek Texts and English Translations of Their Writings*. Edited and revised by M.W. Holmes. Grand Rapids: Baker, 1992.

List, John with Goodrich, Austin. *Collateral Damage: the John List Story*. Lincoln: iUniverse, Inc., 2006.

MacArthur, John F. *The Gospel According to Jesus*. Grand Rapids: Zondervan, 1988.

Marsh, John. *The Fulness of Time*. London: Nisbet, 1952.

Miguel, De La Torre A, and Hernandez, Albert. *The Quest for the Historical Satan*. Minneapolis: Fortress Press, 2011.

Minear, Paul. *Christ Hope and the Second Coming*. Philadelphia: Westminster, 1954.

Moore, Charles E. *Provocations: Spiritual Writings of Kierkegaard*. Farmington: Plough Publishing House, 2002.

Murray, William. *My Life without God*. Eugene: Harvest House, 1992.

Murray-Beasley, George R. *Jesus and the Last Days*. Peabody: Hendrickson, 1993.

Nagel, Myra B. *Deliver Us from Evil*. Cleveland: United Church Press, 1999.

Pentecost, Dwight J. *The Words & Works of Jesus Christ*. Grand Rapids: Zondervan, 1981.

Philips, J.B. *Your God is Too Small*. New York: Macmillan Company, 1961.

Plevnik, Joseph. *Paul and the Parousia*. Peabody: Hendrickson, 1997.

Polkinghorne, John. *Belief in God in an Age of Science*. New Haven and London: Yale University Press, 1998.

Polkinghorne, John. *Quarks, Chaos and Christianity: Questions to Science and Religion*. New York: Crossroad, 1996.

Post, Laurens van der. *A Walk with a White Bushman*. London: Chatto & Windus, 1986.

Reinfenber, A. *Israels's History in Coins*. London: Schocken Books, 1953.

Robinson, William. *The Devil and God*. Nashville: Abingdon-Cokesbury, 1945.

Rogers, Jr., Cleon L. and Rogers, III., Cleon L. *The New Linguistic and Exegetical Key to the Greek New Testament*. Grand Rapids: Zondervan, 1998.

Russell, Bertrand. *Why I Am Not a Christian*. New York: Simon & Schuster, 1957.

Russell, Jeffrey Burton. *A History of Heaven: The Singing Silence*. Princeton: Princeton University Press, 1997.

Russell, Jeffrey Burton. *Lucifer: The Devil in the Middle Ages*. Ithaca and London: Cornell University Press, 1984.

Russell, Jeffrey Burton. *The Prince of Darkness: Radical Evil and the Power of Good in History*. Ithaca and London: Cornell University Press, 1988.

Russell, Jeffrey Burton. *Satan: The Early Christian Tradition*. Ithaca and London: Cornell University Press, 1981.

Schaeffer, Francis A. *Escape from Reason*. Downers Grove: InterVarsity Press, 1978.

Schaeffer, Francis A. *He Is There and He Is Not Silent*. Wheaton: Tyndale House, 1972.

Seaman, Ann Rowe. *America's Most Hated Woman: the Life and Gruesome Death of Madalyn Murray O'Hair*. New York and London: Continuum International Publishing, 2005.

Slaughter, Mike. *Change the World*. Nashville: Abingdon Press, 2010.

Solle, Dorothee. *Thinking about God*. Texas: Trinity Press, 1987.

Strobel, Lee. *The Case for a Creator*. Grand Rapids: Zondervan, 2004.

Sullenberger, Chesley with Zaslow, Jeffrey. *Highest Duty*. New York: William Morrow, 2009.

Swindoll, Charles. *Joseph: a Man of Integrity and Forgiveness*. Nashville: Thomas Nelson, 1998.

Van Til, Cornelius. *Christian Apologetics*. Phillipsburg: Presbyterian and Reformed Pub., 1976.

Walsh, John with Lerman, Philip. *No Mercy*. New York: Pocket Books, 1998.

Woods, William. *The History of the Devil*. New York: G.P. Putnam's Sons, 1973.

Yancey, Philip. *After the Wedding*. Waco: Word Books Publisher, 1976.

Yancey, Philip. *Where is God When It Hurts?* Grand Rapids: Zondervan, 1990.

Young, Brad H. *The Parables*. Massachusetts: Hendrickson, 1998.

Zacharias, Ravi. *The Grand Weaver*. Grand Rapids: Zondervan, 2007.